TABLE OF CONTENTS

INTRODUCTION
CHAPTER 1
   JANUARY
CHAPTER 2
   CELTMAN 2016
CHAPTER 3
   FEBRUARY 2024
CHAPTER 4
   ~~CELTMAN 2020~~ TODDMAN 2020
CHAPTER 5
   MARCH 2024
CHAPTER 6
   CELTMAN 2021
CHAPTER 7
   APRIL
CHAPTER 8
   CELTMAN 2022 – SUPPORT
CHAPTER 9
   MAY
CHAPTER 10
   CELTMAN SOLO POINT FIVE 2023
CHAPTER 11
   JUNE

INTRODUCTION

Celtman is not your average triathlon.

Competitors start with a 3.4km swim in cold, jellyfish-infested water. They then face a 202km bike ride with strong headwinds that can make it feel like they're pedalling backwards. Finally, they conquer a mountain marathon that includes two Munros (Scottish mountains over 3,000 feet) all while being attacked by millions of midges.

Any competitor who manages to complete the course receives a... t-shirt.

A blue T-shirt for those who climb the mountains and a white T-shirt for those who don't. There are no medals. No swag bag, and, not even a free biscuit to feast on at the finish line. It's just a t-shirt and memories.

In this book I will detail my experience, as an average athlete, taking part in this scary, awe-inspiring race. During my training I recorded my thoughts each day.

I hope reading this will inspire you to believe that a challenge like Celtman is possible. I'm just a normal athlete with a family, a busy job and a diet that contains too many sweet treats.

If I can do it then anyone can do it.

CHAPTER 1

JANUARY

MONDAY 1 JANUARY 2024 (REST)

I don't believe in New Year resolutions. Why make a resolution on the first day of January? I am having a day off. I don't want to commit to a resolution whilst I'm enjoying a day off.

For example, creating a resolution to say I won't eat chocolate would be pointless. There's a gigantic box of Quality Street in my kitchen cupboard and I have all day to sit in the house and watch telly. You might as well ask a lemming not to leap off a cliff. It's against nature not to finish a box of chocolates as soon as it's open.

That's why I believe in the New Year + 1 day resolution. It could even be more than +1 day if I include weekends or extra holidays.

This year my resolution will be a simple one - complete Celtman. There's no B-plan. No backup race. My aim is Celtman or nothing.

TUESDAY 2 JANUARY 2024 (REST)

I live in Scotland. I get the 2nd January as a day off. My resolution can wait as I have chocolates to eat.

WEDNESDAY 3 JANUARY 2024 (RESOLUTION)

Resolution set - complete Celtman! I take the rest of the day off from training to celebrate this accomplishment. Mmm... chocolates.

THURSDAY 4 JANUARY 2024 (BIKE/SWIM)

"Doing it for the 'Gram" means doing something – a holiday, breakfast, a selfie – with the primary goal of posting/boasting about it on Instagram. It's less about the actual experience and more about crafting a perfect image. Like enjoying a fancy (and photogenic) breakfast instead of a bowl of corn flakes and milk.

I don't have Instagram but I do now have a Celtman diary so today I am "Doing it for the Celtman Diary." It means doing something because I need to write about it for my diary – even if the desire to record it overshadows the enjoyment of doing it.

I cycled in the morning, and, I squeezed in a swim and some stretching... followed by smashed avocado on toast. I then took a selfie. #smashedit

I would have happily done nothing today but thankfully the need to put something in my diary forced me to exercise.

FRIDAY 5 JANUARY 2024 (RUN)

Today is twelfth night. The day Christmas trees should come down.

I run through the streets near my house to get one last look at the trees before they all come down...except for two houses. These two houses keep them up.

Last year, they didn't take down their trees for months. They waged a Christmas tree war in the name of Christmas spirit... or sheer bloody-mindedness. Who would blink first and take down their tree?

At first, I was understanding. "Maybe they are on holiday," I mused. "Maybe it is an unexpected hospital stay," I reasoned. But as weeks turned into months, those neighbouring trees became defiant monuments. Were they trapped inside by a vengeful Santa? Had a rogue band of elves taken over?

By month three, the only logical explanation was that it was a high-stake bet. However, one of them had a real tree. And as winter retreated, their festive centrepiece turned into a crispy brown fire hazard. Even the cat looked embarrassed as the green tree turned into a festive brown twig before, finally, appearing in a bin outside their house at the start of April. In a final act of spite, in the second house, a fake tree clung on for another fortnight, disappearing in a huff in mid-April. I half expected a "We Won!" banner to take its place.

I get sad when the Christmas lights flicker out. The streets lose their magic in January, my nightly treasure hunt for gaudy displays grinds to a halt, there's nothing to see but the glimpse of someone watching Pointless or The Chase after work. However, if I need to find some Christmas spirit in the coming months at least I know where to look.

SATURDAY 6 JANUARY 2024 (REST)

Today is my daughter's third birthday which meant today was a rest day. I say rest. I mean cake. Today, was very much a cake day. It wasn't without any exercise: I had to lift the cake.

Tomorrow, I will run... to the fridge... for more cake.

SUNDAY 7 JANUARY 2024 (BIKE)

I bought a smart trainer. The marketing blurb is that it will makes any cycling training program fun.

Which meant I need to get a training program. I looked at a few, but Training Peaks seems to require a spreadsheet, and Sufferfest has the word Suffer right in the title, which is the exact opposite of my workout philosophy – the less suffering the better. If they wanted me to try it then they should have called it 'Push Yourself Gently While Watching NetflixFest'.

Instead, I tried Zwift on an iPad linked to my trainer because it promises I won't suffer as Zwift looks like a computer game. I would get to watch a virtual version of myself cycle round New

York's Central Park or the centre of London. It would be like Mario Kart but with me in it and a kart instead of a bike – Andrew Bike.

I try using Zwift but I don't know I'm doing. My wee man on screen was surrounded by other riders. I try to ride round New York's Central Park and keep my speed around 20mph. But that get boring very quickly, and then –

– someone shot past me, and I thought, "follow them!" and then…

– a group formed around me, and I was in a peloton, and we're all doing 25mph, and I'm thinking, "I can't be dropped".

– then I'm climbing a hill, and a message is telling me that if I keep this pace, I'll be in the top 50.

And I think, "Now, I get it!". Zwift is for folk who need a bit of competition to motivate themselves. It's a game of jealousy. Even though you don't know the people around you, you suddenly want to be better than them just because they're real people too. You're no longer training on your own. I'm not just Mario – I'm also racing Luigi – and I want to make him suffer. While also taking it easy, of course.

MONDAY 8 JANUARY 2024 (REST)

Monday is both a rest day and a review day. This marks the 'official' start of my Celtman training. And the first day I will plan training for the week ahead.

Rather than stick to a rigid plan where for example, Tuesday is always a run, or Wednesday is always a Mars bar treat, I'll use every Monday to focus on the week ahead, marking sessions I want to complete and deciding when to do them week by week. This way, my training fits my life – not the other way around. Life comes first, Celtman second.

This week looks to be a breeze since the sessions are the shortest they'll be for six months. Plus, my only 'life event' is a single day working in a different office. Otherwise, it's a normal work and a normal family routine after the fun disruption of the Christmas break.

TUESDAY 9 JANUARY 2024 (RUN)

Turns out, forgetting to bring my shorts to work leads to sartorial compromises. Last night I packed run leggings, but not my shorts. This lunchtime I had planned to run, I briefly considered bailing, but with only one run on the schedule, I went for it

I can feel the wind against my buttocks as I run. It's not much, but it does feel like I'm streaking in public.

It's amazing the difference a missing layer of fabric makes. I feel 'freer' – and colder. And slightly uncomfortable as if I've transgressed by wearing skin-tight leggings to show my bum as I run. Not that anyone is looking. I'm in Larbert on a cold icy January day. No one is out. Until I meet a colleague walking towards me. We greet each other, I run on. We don't mention it again when we see each other later in the day. What happens on the street, stays on the street.

It's apt that clothes feature so highly in my session as I was thinking about clothes when I packed my bag. As a symbolic act, I packed a Celtman t-shirt (and a running jacket, I'm not daft, this is Scotland in January). I wanted to wear the t-shirt to signify this run was different. It was the first training run. The first step to Celtman in June. Now, if only Celtman made shorts, I wouldn't have felt so naked.

WEDNESDAY 10 JANUARY 2024 (BIKE)

My day was like this:

6:30am - wake up alarm
6:45am - on stationary bike

THE CELTMAN DIARY

3pm.- yawning

I rode Zwift's Scotland map. I spot castles everywhere. Its supposed to be Glasgow but its not the Glasgow I know. The real life centre of Glasgow is as flat and castle-less but in Zwift it is now a sunken garden fit for castle. It's as factually accurate as a Donald Trump speech. .

The Scotland course is based on the 2023 UCI World Championship Course. A course I rode last summer. I didn't see any castles or sunken gardens.

Supposedly no one was supposed to ride the course in advance but hypothetically – and, honest, officer, this is purely my imagination – here's how a sneaky pre-race ride might've gone from someone who definitely didn't ride it the morning before the woman's world championship race.

First, the course received some notoriety before the championships began as it had 42 corners and would require the riders to turn almost 500 times during their 12 laps of the course. Not that I counted. I lost count somewhere around turn 367. Did the designers have a surplus to use up?

As for the course marshals, they were very helpful. The first time I went round, they didn't utter a peep. The second time, their cries of "Turn back, you fool!" offered crystal-clear directional insight. I'd taken a wrong turn and was going the wrong way round. Unfortunately, they were less helpful once I did turn when they shouted: "Race in progress, get off!"

The longest climb on the course is Montrose Street, beside Strathclyde University. However, it's not the hardest climb on the course. That would be Scott Street in Garnethill, which is shorter but much steeper. Neither is particularly challenging, at least not at the pace I was going. I imagine it's harder when you're trying to win a World Championship and you're trying to go as fast as you can.

It was great to see the course and to ride through the city without traffic lights or traffic to worry about. There were also no potholes as the council had filled them all the week before.

If you check Strava you'll find that every Strava segment in the course has been claimed by a professional cyclist so if you're looking for records, then you'll need to do what I saw one man do: fastest up Montrose Street on a Brompton bile. I'd love to see Mathieu van der Poel try that one.

But I definitely didn't ride the course and even if you saw me, it wasn't me and that's because when I stopped at George Square, as you couldn't ride through the finish line, a woman walked over and said "Good luck in the race today!".

I was flattered. She must have thought I was a professional. Then I remembered it was the woman's race later and she must have thought I was an international female cyclist. Which was handy, as international female cyclists were permitted to be on the streets.

THURSDAY 11 JANUARY 2024 (SWIM)

6:20AM – My alarm goes off. I leave the house and head to a swimming pool.

7:00AM – I start swimming

8:00AM – I am gubbed! My arms are very tired.

For Celtman, I've re-joined my triathlon club's coached swim sessions. The sessions will push me harder than I'd ever push myself, which is the point. If I can survive these sessions, at least my stamina will be up for the Celtman swim... assuming my arms haven't fallen off first.

Blimey is right. Today was supposed to be a gentle re-introduction. I show up, innocently checking the lane assignments: one for the speed demons, one for... well, the rest of us. Naturally, I assume I'm with the 'rest of us'. Two kilometres and a series of brutal 500-meter repeats later, I'm absolutely gubbed. My arms feel like overcooked noodles.

Turns out, "slower" is a relative term. Maybe next time I'll just bring a snorkel and some flippers and hang out at the bottom of the pool. At least then the lifeguard might have a reason to drag me out of the water.

FRIDAY 12 JANUARY 2024 (RUN)

It's cold outside and I don't want to go out. I give myself a metaphorical kick up the ass (covered in shorts) and go out anyway.

SATURDAY 13 JANUARY 2024 (BIKE)

It's nice outside, and I'm itching to get out. But five minutes into a bike ride, my right-hand gear shifter decides to become a projectile, clanging against the pavement. I'm annoyed, but not surprised. It's not the first time it's fallen off. However, the superglue fix I've used before doesn't appear to have survived three months stored in the shed's winter chill.

As triathletes, we put our faith in technology. Yet, sometimes a flat tire, snapped spoke, or rebellious gear shifter can ruin the best-laid plans. Luckily, I was close to home and could switch to the indoor trainer.

Speaking of tech, you might be wondering what bike I was using. The Celtman bike debate – road or time trial – rages on. And to help you decide, let's talk names. Road bike? Goes on the road. Track bike? Loves the track. Simple enough. But a mountain bike? That's for...well, mountains, possibly with experts in tow. I'm no expert. When purchasing a mountain bike I bought an Orange one.

No, not an Orange brand bike (though they exist). And not one I carefully engineered from citrus fruits. I simply bought an orange coloured one that I liked the look of (without knowing anything about the spec.)

Choosing a bike can be complex. With a road bike, I'd consider aero positions, TT builds... all the things that sound like they make you go faster but I have no idea how they do that. But mountain bikes? That's a world I understand even less. Which must be why I bought a bike with a broken gear shifter. Instead all I considered was:

Wheels: Bigger = cooler? Probably comfier too, like riding on pillows. But the thought of pumping them up made my head spin. I recommend biggish. Not small. Not big. Just biggish. Middle ground is good.

Frame: Suspension or no suspension? I want the cool-looking suspension thingamajigs, even if I never touch them. Purely for the style points.

Front Suspension: Must have a logo that screams "I KNOW WHAT I'M DOING". My suspension said "Rockshock" on the side, which sounds appropriately aggressive, even if it's probably mountain bike slang for something embarrassing.

Saddle: Unless it actively tries to impale me, I'm not bothered. Black is always a safe bet.
Brakes & Gears: Essential. Double-check they exist. Beyond that, I'm lost.

And with this knowledge, I confidently marched into a store and said, "Ooh, that orange one's nice!" as soon as I saw it. Because sometimes, gut feeling beats technical jargon.

SUNDAY 14 JANUARY 2024 (RUN)

Heavy legs to finish the week. I run with my brother to help motivate me to run longer than I would have if I was running on my own. Running with others can help training, particularly with long runs, and particularly when the other person is training for an ultra-marathon.

My brother has entered a track marathon. He will run 26 miles around a track in East Kilbride.

"Can you turn round and run in the other director for a bit of variety?" I asked.

"Of course not," he said, "I would be running backwards."

MONDAY 15 JANUARY 2024 (REST)

There are many ways that you can injure yourself. Some are obvious: ice on a road when riding your bike; a hole in the pavement to twist your ankle while running. Others are less so. Footballer Kirk Broadfoot certainly didn't expect to injure himself cooking an egg in a microwave, but, when it exploded, he missed his next match. Food should come with a health warning – especially when you're stretching.

For the last two nights I've tried to stretch shortly after large meals. I didn't think anything of it. I know not to swim on a full stomach or to run while stuffed full of biscuits, but I didn't expect it to have any effect on my stretching. I was wrong.

While stretching out was fine – reaching up, extending arms and legs, anything that involved length – as soon as I start to curl, whether doubling over or crunching up – I felt like I was jumping on a bag pipe in my stomach. "OOOHHHHHAAAAHHHHAWGGHHHHH!" I went, just like the lovely sound of a bag pipe. There are certain moves that you can't do with a full stomach.

I guess this should be obvious. You can't eat two hot dogs, chips, and a chip butty and a yoghurt (because I'm being healthy) and expect it to go from plate to stomach and to vanish on the way. My stomach is full of the food I've just eaten. It doesn't disappear in 30 minutes. Digestion takes time. That's why I share this warning: the only thing you should stretch after a large meal is your waistband.

TUESDAY 16 JANUARY 2024 (BIKE)

I decide to bike first thing in the morning. To help, I set up the bike before I went to bed last night. Towel on handlebars, water bottle filled, iPad charged. I even take out a t-shirt and cycle shorts and place them beside my shoes, so I don't need to think about getting changed. That way my alarm goes off at 635, I shuffle out of bed at 640, into clothes and on bike by 645. I can then cycle until shower, breakfast, and train at 820 a.m.

WEDNESDAY 17 JANUARY 2024 (FAIL)

I run regularly at lunchtime from our office in Larbert. I usually prepare my bag the night before, so I have my kit, my towel, a change of clothes and my trainers.

Normally, I'm a Boy Scout. Be prepared. Except, I wasn't a very good Boy Scout two weeks ago nor today nor last year when I forgot the most important item of all. Not my towel, there's always ways to dry off even if you forget a towel, including but not limited to a roll of toilet paper, which we shall never speak about. Nor did I forget my shorts. That was last week's folly. Instead, the worst item you can forget is a fresh pair of socks. Once you've been running, you don't want to wear your socks again. They need to be banished into the darkest deepest parts of your bag so that the smell is smothered until you fish them out later with a pair of tongs to throw them in the washing machine.

But if you have no socks, what do you do? Nothing. You can't wear loo roll on your feet. Nor can you colour in your ankles with a black marker and pretend you've got socks on.
Instead, you have no choice but to dress like an 18-year-old trying to get into a nightclub, ankles flashing on too short trousers.

I had to spend the rest of my day making sure not to leave my desk so that no one could accuse me, a 46-year-old man, of being some kind of Hoxton Hipster from 2015.

"Is that your ankles I can see?" Someone would ask.

And I had to explain that I work in social media marketing and as a part time barista and that this was a uniform, not a choice.

So, from them on, to avoid it happening again I have a pair of emergency socks in my bag. That way if I ever forget to bring a pair I can break out the emergency socks so that I can walk freely again without showing off my ankles.

But emergency socks are no good when you forget your shorts. Or when you forget your running jacket, like I did today. And while I brought my running kit to work so I could run home, I forgot to bring a jacket. With temperatures hovering between minus three and minus my bollocks because they'd freeze off if I venture outside, I didn't fancy running home in just a thin t-shirt. This meant I could do anything because by the time I got home I didn't have any time to do anything else.

THURSDAY 18 JANUARY 2024 (SWIM)

To make sure I arrive on time, I set my alarm for 6:15 AM for a 7:00 AM swim session. Of course, my traitorous brain wakes me up at 5:30 AM, fully alert and completely resistant to any further sleep. So, in a display of questionable judgement, I haul myself out of bed, down a breakfast fit for a lumberjack, and arrive at the pool 10 minutes early... only to stare at the still-locked doors.

FRIDAY 19 JANUARY 2024 (BIKE)

Two and a half hours on an indoor bike. I'm not sure if I should be laughing, crying, or calling an ambulance. My legs are jelly, my lungs are burning, and my brain is begging for sweet, sweet release.

But I can't stop. I won't stop. Because I'm a glutton for punishment, apparently.

Chris Hoy had a mattress to collapse onto after his sprint

sessions. I have a puddle of sweat and a growing sense of existential dread.

Normally, I'd do this kind of thing on the weekend when I have time to recover and/or wallow in self-pity. But today is Friday, and I'm fresh off the clock.

I've never cycled indoors for this long before. I'm not sure if I'm setting a new world record or just proving that I'm a complete and utter masochist. To get through it, I started with YouTube. Then I moved onto a book. Then I started watching paint dry. Anything to distract me from the pain and the suffering.

And now, as I sit here on the floor, my legs shaking uncontrollably, I can't help but wonder: what the hell am I doing with my life?

SATURDAY 20 JANUARY 2024 (SWIM/RUN) & SUNDAY 21 JANUARY 2024 (BIKE)

And by the next day, I'm a walking testament to the phrase "no rest for the wickedly fit". Sure, I took my daughter swimming, but did I simply watch from the sidelines like a sane parent? Of course not. Mrs Celtwife took her home, and I seized the golden opportunity – a 1km swim is basically a warmup, right? Might as well tack on a casual jog home, just for kicks.

This is what Celtman does to you. One day, you're asking "why am I doing this?" and the next day you're asking "why am I doing more?".

Today's session should be named the 'And then I ran/biked home because I'm clearly insane'" session. With my schedule, the only way to squeeze in a workout is by creatively weaving it around other tasks. Need groceries? Better bike to the shops and carry them home in my backpack. Visiting relatives? Best jog there to burn off the inevitable stress-eating later.

The problem with the '...ran home' session is that it misses out the crucial words "... ran home... while tired". Though even that doesn't cut it. It's more like "... ran home delirious and contemplating faking my own death to escape the pain."

You can avoid the '... ran home' session by not leaving your home in the first place. On Sunday, with Storm Isha predicated to bring in heavy rain and strong winds, I stayed indoors and cycled instead.

I was meant to be taking part in a race: the Nigel Barge 10k, which, with Storm Isha's help, would have definitely set a new personal best.

Instead, I still race, but this time on Zwift. Racing on Zwift is a great way to keep your motivation up when training indoors. Not only do you get all the normal race feelings of "I've not prepared for this", "why is everyone faster than me" and "Dear God, why did I enter this?" but it's warm, so you don't mind (as much).

Today, I entered a race involving Zwift's biggest climb, Alpe Du Zwift, the digital version of Alpe Du Huez.

I've been to Alpe Du Huez. I saw the Tour De France and walked from the base of the climb to corner seven so I know exactly what it's like to go very slowly up a very big climb.

And, though I'm basing this on memories of a hot French day, the climb in Zwift seems to be a very faithful version of the real climb, even down to the Scotsman at the side of the road walking up and wondering if he's brought enough water for five hours on the side of a mountain. (He hadn't).

Entering races on Zwift is fun and does give a sense of achievement missing from a normal session – unless your normal session always finishes with a lap round the house, arms aloft and shouting "Championee!" in which case, well done you!

MONDAY 22 JANUARY 2024 (REST)

"That ain't right" are not words you don't want to hear in the middle of a check up, and while just wearing a pair of pants.

I was in the middle of my annual physio M.O.T. Every year, I go back to the same physio for 45 minutes of prodding and poking to check my posture and balance.

Usually this involves an elbow, some gasps (mine), and a great feeling of relaxing and easing of aches and pains. It should relax me, not create anxiety.

"That's definitely not right," she said again, poking my chest.

"What's not right?" I thought, my hypochondriac mind thinking of a hundred different ways that checking whether one leg is longer than the other could be a sign of Ebola or the Black Death.

"Did you break a rib?" She asked.

"No," I thought, but after all her prodding and poking with her elbow to relieve muscles tension in my back I wouldn't have been surprised if she'd broken one at the start of the check up. Her hands could knock down a wall faster than a wrecking ball.

"Because your ribs have shifted to the right." She explained.

And then I remembered that while I may not have broken a rib, I gave it a good crack last year while trying and failing to jump across a river at Torridon, the finishing point of Celtman. At the time, I'd didn't go and see a doctor because I knew he would have just said to rest up and let it heal. A cracked rib is one of those injuries that only time can cure.

"Let's put it back in place," she said, before proceeding to crack the right ribs so hard they were pushed back to the left.

Sometimes the cure is worse than the illness.

While runners and athletes often shrug off injuries, it's always worth going to see a physio to find out if the injuries are causing any other problems. It turned out I was leaning further right than Nigel Farage standing on the White Cliffs of Dover and pointing at France. Small niggles can lead to bigger problems. And, if you can, and you have the opportunity, I'd recommend getting a regular check up from a physio. Even a psychotic one.

TUESDAY 23 JANUARY 2024 (BIKE)

I should have been running today but Storm Jocelyn has arrived and I'm worried that if I run in the right direct, with the wind at my back, I could easily break the speed limit. And if I flap your arms at the same then I could take off too.

But then add rain into the mix, I really don't fancy running outside in the middle of a gale while buckets of a water are thrown in my face. Now some people may say that:

"Andrew, you're training for an extreme triathlon, these are the very conditions you should want to train in to prove that you are an EXTREME athlete".

To them, I say, "I've entered a race, a one day race, not a six month endurance event. Did Bear Grylls spend all day outdoors eating bull testicles or did he spend the night in a hotel in-between filming? That's right: he spent the night in a hotel. Just as I want to spend today in my spare room, sitting on my bike, in a warm dry room. And if that make me less EXTREME then so be it."

WEDNESDAY 24 JANUARY 2024 (BIKE AGAIN)

Peter Sagan. Mark Cavendish. Andrew Todd. What do we all have in common? We've all cycled round the Arc de Triomphe in Paris with a green jersey on our back. Of course, they have the much more prestigious Green Jersey for highest points at the Tour Du France. Mine was for getting up first thing and riding the Paris course on Zwift while no one else was racing, making me the fastest rider on the course (the only rider on the course). But who's counting the differences? I'm a Green Jersey champion in

Paris!

It's a good tip for anyone chasing records either virtually on Zwift or other virtual worlds or, even in the real world, by chasing the records on Strava for fastest person to race a particular segment. If you're first, you can be first.

My brother is always the fastest person each year to ride the Crow Road segment on Strava. The Crow Road is a hill behind Lennoxtown, a town just north of Glasgow, and which formed part of the UCI World Championship Course in 2023. As my brother lives in Lennoxtown, on 1 January he gets up while it's still dark and cycles to the top of the Crow Road so that no matter how fast or slows he cycles, he'll be the fastest person to ride the Crow Road that year – as he's the only and first person to ride it.

The same thing works in Zwift. First thing in the morning, choose a world with few riders, and you too can be a champion.

THURSDAY 25 JANUARY 2024 (SWIM)

From champion to last place but it wasn't my fault. Near the end of the swim session, I noticed the nose bridge in my googles was start to break. There was a tear through three quarters of it and it was only hanging together by a thin strip of rubber. I hoped it would last as we started our final set – 400m – but as I reached the end of the pool at 200m, it snapped, and I got whacked in the face by the separated goggles exploding on the end of my nose before my eyeballs were bleached by the chlorine of the pool. Ouch. Yikes.

I'm not sure what would happen if my goggles split during the Celtman split. The salt water would make continuing difficult. Calling a support boat might be the only option. I can only hope that it won't happen again as, after years of swimming, this is the first time it has happened to me.

FRIDAY 26 JANUARY 2024 (BIKE)

THE CELTMAN DIARY

If you think a layer is where James Bond gets captured, then today was for you. I don't understand layers. I understand keeping warm and keeping dry. I'm Scottish, keeping warm and keeping dry are basic life skills in Glasgow. But layering is different. It suggests that if you wear the right amount of clothes then you'll reach an optimum temperature where you are neither too warm or too cold. That's just crazy talk. There's no such thing as too warm. You can always be warmer in Scotland.

The Scots must be the only people in the world who invented a hot drink in one of the world's hottest regions. Darjeeling in India is famous for its tea. But Darjeeling tea plantations were created in the 18th century, in part by a Scotsman, as it could only be a Scot who'd think that a country where the temperature routinely hits the mid 30s was missing a boiling cup of water.

However, if you read running magazines and look on-line, you'll find hundreds of products that claim to wick away sweat (where does it go?), helps your body breathe (my mouth does that) while wrapping it in the finest merino (didn't he manage Chelsea?) wool.

I don't believe in any of that. At least not in Winter. Especially in Scottish Winter. In Winter you need to keep warm and the only way to do that is to cover your body in the most inefficient man-made fibres known to man. When I go running, I want to come back, strip off and feel like I've just experienced a tropical storm in a sleeping bag. I want to feel like my clothes need a tumble dry before I wash them. In short, the cheaper the t-shirt the better it is for winter running. Too hot? There's no such thing.

That's why I want to sing the praise of Decathlon. For £2.99 they produce the finest (worst) base layer known to man. It doesn't breathe. It doesn't wick. It barely fits (buy a size bigger than you think). It's useless at keeping you cool – but it's perfect at keeping you warm.

I have five.

Just as I have five cycle shorts from them too. I don't see the point on spending money on expensive shorts for cycling indoors.

Until today.

I will buy better cycle shorts when cycling for longer than an hour.

SATURDAY 27 JANUARY 2024 (SWIM)

I should go for a run today, but my legs are heavy after yesterday. I go for a swim instead.

I know I should train to run on heavy legs because running while tired is good preparation for running the final part of a normal long-distance triathlon. But sometimes you just have to listen to your body and my body said "nah, not today."

SUNDAY 28 JANUARY 2024 (RUN)

I'm running with Iain Celtbrother as he trains for his track marathon. I don't see the attraction in running a marathon around a running track. Over 100 circuits of a 400m track again and again and again and again. The repetition would destroy me.

It's only later that I realise that my life is nothing but repetition. Swim. Bike. Run. Repeat. I shouldn't be so quick to criticise others for something that only takes four hours when I face six months of repetition.

That's why I'm not rigid about sticking to a plan and am happy to change things for weather, like earlier in the week or through tiredness, like yesterday. I will have plenty of time to run, and to swim and to swim cycle in the next six months.

MONDAY 29 JANUARY 2024 (REST DAY)

Monday is a rest day but that doesn't mean I can rest. I have a dog, Barney, and he still needs walking. Every night we walk 30 mins to an hour ad normally he leads the way. He decides which directions to go when we leave the house and walks tend to develop from there. Except for the last two weeks. Instead, all walks are dictated by random women throughout the UK. Mrs Celtwife has sold some old clothes on Vinted, an app that specialises in selling clothes.

Each time Mrs Celtwife makes a sale, the buyer can select from several options, including InPost, Evri and RoyalMail. Depending on what option they choose we have to drop off the clothes in a separate location. So now, instead of asking Barney where he wants to go, we're dropping parcels off instead.

"Where will we go tonight?"

"Well, Sandra from Ipswich has selected Evri for her pink blouse from Reiss so that means we're going to Tesco."

But the next night:

"Cheryl from Maidstone wants InPost. We need to go to the BP garage!"

I assume this is what it's like to use an online coach. You know what you need to do – run, bike, swim or, in our case, walk the dog – but how you do it is completely controlled by a stranger on the internet.

TUESDAY 30 JANUARY 2024 (REST)

I always have a yoghurt at lunchtime. Today, in Tesco, I spotted a caramel yoghurt that said it contained 18g of protein. After three weeks of training, I thought it would be good to add some additional protein to my diet and the easiest way to do that would be to try this new pot. It was a nice idea but when "protein" is in bigger letters than "caramel", it should have been a hint about how strongly the manufacturer was concerned about flavour.

"Athletes don't need flavour – they need results!"

Not this athlete. The yoghurt was a shiny brown colour that can only be described as "shiny shite" and a taste that can also be described as "shiny shite". As for the texture, well, you know where this joke is going...

No training today. Mrs Celtwife had to work through the night and then go to work in the morning, so I dropped her off and picked her up to save her falling asleep on a train.

WEDNESDAY 31 JANUARY 2024 (RUN)

Why am I doing this? What's the point? Do I have to continue to do this day after day after day? But enough about writing this diary, what about the training?

The first couple of weeks are novel.

I'm training, I tell myself.

This is important, I justify.

But, after three weeks, I start to think, not again. Why can't I just take a day off? And then I run home, I run an extra couple of miles, I look at my watch and I see I've am running faster than normal but without any extra effort. Training works. And it's nights like tonight that I realise why I do this: to improve.

Or it could be that I ran home at the tail end of a storm and the wind was pushing me along, giving me a boost.

Possibly.

But I like to believe that maybe, just maybe, I was running faster because I've been training.

CHAPTER 2

CELTMAN 2017

Damn.

That's all I could say to that.

Damn.

In 2016, I entered three race ballots. The first ballot was for a race which I didn't want to race. But I did want to increase my chances to enter it in the future as every entry and failure to be selected gave additional chances in future race ballots.

And I was successful. Not because I was selected. But, because I was not selected, which was the selection I wanted, if you know what I mean. I won by losing.

The second ballot was a place in Celtman. And this one I wanted to win. And I did by winning, not losing, and being lucky enough to be selected to race in 2017.

And the third ballot was for a place in the Escape From Alcatraz triathlon. A triathlon that started with a swim form Alcatraz prison in San Francisco.

This ballot entry was a long shot. A 'I'll never get in but might as well enter because you never know' race. There were only 2,000 places and there were 10s of thousands of entries. I had no hope of getting in... until I got in.

Damn.

Escape From Alcatraz was a once in a lifetime race. A chance to jump off a ferry beside Alcatraz island (they can't start on the island because of the current) and to swim back to shore next to the Golden Gate Bridge. An 18 mile closed road bike circuit and a 8 mile run follow. All in San Francisco – a city I'd always wanted to visit.

But there was a problem. A Celtman shaped problem.

Escape From Alcatraz was the week before Celtman. It would be silly to try and do both, wouldn't it? I would be tapering for Celtman, not taking part in a triathlon halfway across the world.

But...

...could I just take it easy. Use the swim as good practice and use the bike and run as gentle exercises?

But...

...what about jetlag? I would just have returned from the States. I once flew eight hours overnight to London, then had a four hour wait before a connecting flight to Glasgow. I was awake for nearly 36 hours after getting up at 10am (UK time) in the States and not going to bed until 10pm on Tuesday. I could barely muster the energy to walk never mind swim three miles, cycle 120 and run a marathon around Beinn Eighe.

But...

I wanted to do both.

But...

Can I do both? Should I do both? Hence...

Damn.

But in the end, it was an easy choice. I knew I couldn't do both so chose to take part in Escape from Alcatraz instead. A race that that didn't start well.

"Have you got the key?" My wife asked.

"Yes," I said, closing the door to our AirBnB flat in San Francisco.

I patted my pocket.

Nothing.

"Wait a minute…"

I tried the door. It was locked.

"When I said I had the key…"

This was not how today was meant to begin. Ater crashing out soon after we arrived, this day was our chance to explore the city and, after waking at 2am, then 3am, then getting up at 4am due to the jet lag, we were ready to pop out at 7am and get breakfast when the nearest shop opened.

"Are you taking your phone?"

"No, I won't need it."

"Are you taking your wallet?"

"I've got cash."

"Have you got the keys?"

"Of course!"

I didn't.

It was 7am. We were trapped outside our flat and the only thing to do was to sit on a children's swing outside and wonder if the ladder in the sculptor's studio (don't ask) next to our flat would extend to the first-floor window we'd left open.

I could see myself reaching through the window, sliding in and opening the door.

I could see myself getting shot by a policeman for breaking and entering.

I ditched the ladder plan.

I had a better plan!

We would use the cash to get a train to the city centre to find an Apple store with free internet access and computers ready to use.

They say the computers are for sale, but everyone knows an Apple store is just a pretentious internet café. We would then send an email to our landlords and get spare keys from them.

It was full proof/fool proof. Except we didn't know how to get a train or get to the city centre or find an Apple store.

But that's what true grit is all about.

Bear Grylls would be proud.

Using our guile, guts and ingenuity we wondered the streets until we spotted a station, then wondered the city centre until we spotted some 'posh shops' then narrowed down our search to a few blocks on the basis that Apple always has a shop in the posh part of town.

Bear Grylls may follow rivers to find his escape, we followed Gucci, Tiffanys and Luis Vuitton.

I could have my own adventure TV show in which I show how luxury items can be used to help survive difficult locations – which, to be honest, is no different to Bear's shows and his secret luxury caravan but at least I'd be honest about it.

Five hours later, after a ride in a cable car and a Pain Au Chocolat in the world famous Tartine Bakery, after such hard, harsh, desperate struggles, we finally got into our flat and I could only hope that escaping from Alcatraz was easier than breaking into an AirBnB.

"Athletes, listen, this is an important announcement! You must – "

Pfffffftt. Ziiipppp. Fffffuutttt. PA broken. Silence.

I was waiting in transition. I was wearing a wetsuit and trainers. I should have been swimming in San Francisco bay but I'm not – the 2017 Escape From Alcatraz swim has been cancelled (for the first time ever!) and I'm waiting to find out what happens next.

It was an early start, 4am alarm, but, with the time difference between UK and the US it still felt like mid-morning. I got an Uber to transition, having left my bike there yesterday, the first time they've let people rack up on the Saturday. I didn't know at this point it wasn't the only weekend 'first'.

At transition I had plenty of time to set up my gear (unroll towel, check bike helmet, 10 seconds, done), check bike for air (press both tyres down with my thumb, 5 seconds each) and then catch a bus to the boat which takes me out to Alcatraz (just a couple of minutes to catch the bus).

The last bus leaves at 6am but, as I wasn't sure of queues, I'd arrived at transition early and after completing my rigorous and thorough transition routine... I was on the bus by 5am, which was too early. I was on the boat by 5:30 and had two hours to wait until the swim start.

On the boat, a former sternwheeler (I Googled this), you get divided by age: over 40 onto the top deck, under 40 on the main deck. In case you forget how old you are you can check your leg: at registration they write your age in black marker on your left hamstring.

I was under 40, and with my memory intact, I don't even need to check when asked, so I got to sit on the main desk. As I'm there early, there's plenty of places to sit, so I sat down.

"Sorry, you can't sit there."

The man to my left was indicating an empty space of 10 metres.

"My friend is just coming back." He said.

"It's okay, I'm sure we'll both fit."

I sat down and then worried that a man with a 10 metre wide butt will sit on me. Luckily, when the friend returned, he had a normal size butt – as do the two others who later joined us. Not that I was checking out their butts. But how much room does one butt need?! Even Sir Mix-A-Lot, the world's foremost expert on big butts and a man who cannot lie, would have said there was room for plenty of butts on that part of the boat.

I closed my eyes. Listened to random conversation and thought about the swim.

I'm nervous. Scared. But I had a secret weapon. The previous night I left a water bottle in the fridge and I plan to pour it on my face and down my back before jumping into the bay. I think the cold water will help me acclimatise before I plunge in.

But, I never get to check that theory. At 6:30am, just as we're due to sail to the start, a man with a loudspeaker tells us to be quiet and to listen to the PA. The PA then tells us that there's been a "small craft advisory warning "and that the "swim is cancelled".

There's a loud groan. A protest. We're asked to leave the boat and it's still not clear why.

People talk about refunds. About ditching the whole event. One man says he can't run or ride a bike, the only reason he was here was for the swim. Others talk in foreign languages. People travelling around the world to be here. And the swim, the iconic swim from Alcatraz back to San Francisco is cancelled.

Now I know how Al Capone must have felt – there was no escape from Alcatraz today.

Later, I find out that the wind and current was too strong even for the safety boats. The small craft warning was a warning that the kayaks and paddle boards who marshal the swim would not cope with the conditions. And if it was too dangerous for the safety boats it was too dangerous for swimmers.

I was disappointed. I'd travelled a quarter of the world to be here but I know safety comes first. And, after seeing the bay later that day, with whitecaps heading east, rather than west, against the current, and with winds hitting 35mph, it was the right call.

We queued to get back on the buses. It was nearly two hours to get everyone back to transition. We still don't know what's happening, but announcements said that a duathlon (bike and run) race will take place and details will follow.

I kept warm by staying in my dry wetsuit. I thought of pouring the frozen water on my head just so I could have the Alcatraz experience but that would have been a stupid idea.

At transition, the PA fizzles out just as the announcement of the new race is made: "Athletes, listen, this is an important announcement – you must –"

We gather at the entrance instead as a loudspeaker is found. The organisers will send us out in waves. Pros first then by number, five at a time, every 10 seconds, to ensure people are spread out along the course just as they would be if they'd completed the swim.

I finally got to take off my wetsuit and got ready to... ESCAPE FROM TRANSITION.

The rest of the race was short but fun. One good bit was inventing a new game to keep me occupied during the run.

At registration everyone has their age written on their left hamstring with a black marker. I don't know why. Maybe the sharks in the bay want to know how old a leg is before they bite it off?

But, as I ran, I would check out people's legs to see how old they were. Then when they passed, I have a quick sideways look to see if they look older, younger or spot on.

It was basically a very judgemental version of Bruce Forsyth's Play Your Card Rights. Higher! Lower! Blimey, see a doctor, you've had a hard life!

The finish line had a large crowd but the crowd was very quiet. Mrs Celtwife was waiting, and she said afterwards that people in the crowd only cheered athletes they knew rather than everyone as they came in. She also overheard the following conversation which seems relevant to anyone thinking of taking part in any race, but also an important reminder to anyone taking part in an extreme challenge like Celtman.

"C'mon children, let's get ready to cheer Daddy!" Said the Mum.

"Why?" Asked a small child.

"Because he's just finished a big race and it's a massive achievement!" Explained the Mum.

"Is it?" Asked the child.

There was a long pause before the Mum said: "Well, he thinks it is."

CHAPTER 3

FEBRUARY 2024

THURSDAY 1 FEBRUARY 2024 (RUN)

When buying a Christmas present people say it's the thought that counts. Which is true, unless your thought is "this will do!" – then you need to think again and stop being so lazy.

Last year, at the office Christmas party, I was given a book called "Hitler: His Rise To Power" as a Secret Santa present. As I had neither expressed a previous interest in history or proclaimed to my colleagues that I was going to extend my desk by annexing a break-out room, I could only think this was some kind of message.

I started wondering if I'd displayed any Hitler like tendencies in the office and I had to admit that after some considerable soul searching and reflection of my despotic moments... I WAS NOTHING LIKE HITLER.

It was only later that I discovered that the book was from someone who'd heard I liked reading and they had a book on their bookshelf they'd never read because... THEY DIDN'T LIKE HITLER TOO.

Top tip for Christmas – if giving Hitler as a gift, please make sure the recipient really, really likes Hitler. You might be surprised at how many people don't want Hitler as a Christmas present. (Most of them).

But Christmas isn't just about presents. It's also about training because nothing says "I'm a serious athlete" than training on Christmas Day even though going for a run on Christmas Day is the worst day of the year for running. The 200 calories lost are quashed by the 2,000 calories consumed as eating's not cheating when you've been sprinting.

Despite its lack of any physical benefits, the Christmas Day run is a good mental boost. For the last 15 years I've run on Christmas Day because of a quote from Daley Thomson, the Olympic gold medal winning decathlete. He said he would always train on Christmas Day because he knew his main rivals would all take the day off. He was one day better than everyone else. So, I'd run on Christmas Day and I too would be one day better than everyone else (Daley Thomson excepted).

However, in researching this entry, I found the actual quote from Daley Thomson, and it turned out I'd been doing it all wrong. He said: "Train <u>twice</u> on Christmas Day. Your competitors may only train once." Which means I've only been training the same amount as everyone else. No wonder I never got to the Olympics.

However, I am going to Celtman and today, even though it was not Christmas Day, I trained twice. Once, first thing in the morning. And then again, a couple of hours later. I had a long ride planned but I only had a few hours split between family time to get it in. Rather than reduce the training, I did part as soon I got up, when Mrs Celtwife takes care of potty, breakfast, and getting dressed... and does the same for Celtchild. And a second longer ride when the two of them were away for a few before lunch.

I may not be going to the Olympics but I am deluded enough to think that today was an Olympic achievement.

FRIDAY 2 FEBRUARY 2024 (BIKE)

Today I rode a mountain on Zwift, which is like riding a mountain in real life but without a nice view. I decided to put on a YouTube video showing the summit of Everest so it feels like I achieved something.

SATURDAY 3 FEBRUARY 2024 (REST)

I had a Christmas lunch to attend today. I'm not sure if it counts as being late or early but I do know wearing a paper crown on my head in February gets a lot of strange looks from other diners.

Daley Thomson can help you train on Christmas Day but he has nothing to say about planning training around Christmas lunch. Instead, today's lesson was from a colleague who had two surprise birthday parties after turning 50 last week.

"Last Friday, my wife and parents invited me to a wine tasting. We'd been before so I was looking forward to some cheese and wine. But when we got there, and the door opened, there were 40 friends in the room and a surprise party."

"Did you get some cheese?" I asked, curious whether the original invitation was fake.

"Now you mention it," he said, "no, I didn't."

That seemed unfair. You should never organise a surprise party by telling someone they are doing something else entirely. They might be looking forward to cheese and biscuits and next thing they know they've got nothing to eat, and they must make small talk with 40 friends for the rest of the night. You should always tell people if you have something on. Just like with training. If my lunch had been a surprise, I'd have been annoyed that I couldn't go for a run or spend time on my bike. But, as I knew about it, I'd planned and made sure I had no training planned so I could eat as much cheese as I wanted.

SUNDAY 4 FEBRUARY 2024 (BIKE)

Not quite a storm today but enough of a bad forecast to make training on the bike indoors the only option. Zwift, it was.

I like all the Zwift maps except for one: New York. I don't know why I don't like it. I love London because it reminds me of living there and running around the streets it covers. Yet, despite loving New York, I don't get the same nostalgic feeling of "I've been there". Maybe it's the floating sky bridge, which, as far as I can remember (it's been 15 years since I was in New York), doesn't float above Central Park. Maybe it's new?

One of my favourite things about Zwift is the ability to choose worlds so that I can avoid New York when it appears. And, today,

I could choose a tour of Japan instead of Manhattan or risk the icy pavements and roads of Glasgow. Hopefully, one day, I'll get to see these Japanese roads in real life too. And, a floating sky bridge. Which, if it's going to be anywhere, is sure to be somewhere in the Far East.

Closer to home, there is an option in Zwift to ride part of the Bealach na Ba, which has the highest ascent of any road in the UK, some alpine like 180 degree corners, and which forms part of the Celtman Solo Point Five route. Celtman Solo Point Five being the middle-distance version of Celtman, which, while half the distance of the main race, has more climbing purely because athletes must ride up the Bealach na Ba as part of the bike course.

MONDAY 5 FEBRUARY (REST)

I know that resting again may seem like too much rest given I also rested two days last week but it's important to stick to your training schedule and would it not be worse to break my training by training than to complete my training by not training? If you know what I mean.

Instead, while checking the Celtman forum on Facebook, I am reminded about one of the dangers of Celtman – the swarms of jellyfish in Loch Sheildaig.

"What can we do to avoid getting stung by a jellyfish?" Someone asks.

I know what to do. I have a plan.

Some people get survival tips from a TV adventurer Bear Grylls. A man who hides his luxury caravan hidden just out of shot. Other people get their tips from Ray Mears, a man who tries to avoid being bitten by snakes but whose very name is an anagram of "Ar! My Arse!". Me, I get my survival tips from 90s sitcom Friends.

There's not many 90s sitcoms that you can turn to for survival tips. Frasier could help you charm a maître-d. Only Fools & Horses warns about the dangers of leaning against a wine bar. But only Friends could help you in the wild, and by wild, I mean beach. And, by beach, I mean tourist beach, with lifeguards and flags to warn you before you go for a swim. Also ice cream. And cocktails. And a lounger and free towels.

In Friends, six friends, hence the title of the programme, in case you've not seen it, go the beach. One of the friends is stung by a jellyfish and another of the friends suggests they, ahem, relieve themselves on the spot where it stings as, ahem, urine, ahem, is a cure for jelly fish stings.

Now, you have to ask yourself how this cure was first discovered. Who's first thought was "I know, let's piss on it!" and, having found success in combatting jellyfish, did they try and expand?

"I have a headache, does anyone have any aspirin?"

"No need, I know what to do – let's stand on a chair and piss on your head!"

"I've broken my leg; can someone call an ambulance?"

"Save yourself a phone call – I've got a better idea – let's piss on it!"

In Friends that's exactly what they do. They piss on the friend with the jellyfish sting and, lo and behold, the friend is cured. Or at least I think that's what happens. I've not seen this episode in years so I can't absolutely say that there is an episode of Friends where five friends form a circle and piss on the sixth. I can imagine that happening in Seinfeld, but somehow it doesn't seem right for Friends. Perhaps they all did it into a cup and then it was poured on delicately.

Anyway, however they did it, whether circle splashed or applied from a pot, that episode of Friends stuck in my mind, and I've always known what to do when a jellyfish stings.

I was swimming off South Beach in Miami (which, with its loungers, cocktails, warm water and dusky heat is ideal training for the cold sharp Scottish water of Celtman) when I felt small electric shocks along my arm. I knew I was stung but I wasn't sure by what. I could feel an itchiness and knew I had to swim back to shore and speak to the lifeguard but all I could think was "Is he going to piss on it?"

I'd seen Friends, I knew what happened next.

I climbed the lifeguards' tower, showed him my arm, now turning blotchy red, and said "I think I've been stung."

He said "It's a jellyfish, let me get something for that."

And he grabbed a bottle.

While part of me thought how good it was that he prepared for this emergency by bottling himself in advance, another part of me thought "Please let it be something else, please let it be anything else".

"It's vinegar," he said, spraying the liquid on my outstretched arm.

I sniffed.

I smelt chips.

I realized I was the chips.

It was vinegar.

Vinegar is a cure for jellyfish.

Thank you, Jesus!

Now I can tell Iain CeltBrother he doesn't need a special water bottle to help at transition or that the only place he can go to the toilet is my left arm. Instead, along with the gels, energy bards and high energy drinks, he just needs a bottle of Saxo vinegar – filled with pish.

TUESDAY 6 FEBRUARY (RUN)

This week, I have a race on Sunday, the Kirkintilloch 12.5k, which is notable as one of the best races to spot the difference between two types of runners. There are runners who park beside the start line and then there's runners who park on Mars – to give themselves more of a challenge by running 55 million kilometres as 'warm up'.

I'm a runner who parks beside the start line. If I had a choice, I'd park on the start line. Warming up is just wasted energy after all.

Why run before you need to run?!?

Some people – coaches, athletes and professionals – will tell you that warming up is an essential part of the whole running experience. If you don't warm up then your muscles are cold and stiff and more likely to break. But those people – those experts – have clearly never had to warm up in Scotland in January when it's cold and wet and miserable and the thought of spending 30 seconds stretching each hamstring is as enticing as sharing a hot tub with Donald Trump.

Scotland is not a country for warming up. It's a country for running as fast as you can out your front door until you run as fast as you can back in your front door and straight into a hot shower.

WEDNESDAY 8 FEBRUARY 2024 (BIKE)

The Greggs session. Safe. Reliable. Dull. No effort involved. Just like picking up a sausage roll from Greggs. You know you could do better; you know that if you went anywhere else you would do better, but some days you can't do more than Greggs.

That was today on the bike. I was awake at 515am as Mrs Celtwife had a train to catch. I tried to sleep until 6am but then got up and jumped - though jumped suggests more effort than I actually made, - I eased myself onto the bike and did the bare minimum to tick off a bike session today. I did it. Bike done. But, just like Greggs, I was left with regret and a small sweat.

THURSDAY 9 FEBRUARY 2024 (SWIM)

I watched the BBC show Would I Lie To You last night and one of the contestants tried to convince the panel that they didn't use an alarm clock to wake up, instead they would lie down in their bed, then tap their head against the pillow for each hour of the alarm. A 6am start would be see them tap their head six time before sleep.

"And does it work?" Rob Brydon asked.

"50/50," they said.

I use my phone to wake up for the swim session. Our alarm is normally set for 6.35am but, to get to the pool for 7am, I need to leave at 6.35am. I try not to disturb Mrs Celtwife by using my phone as an alarm but normally I wake up before and switch it off.

I've never tapped my head but I naturally wake up before the alarm. However, I'm not going to rely on that. The first time I don't use my phone, I will inevitably sleep in and I don't want to have to explain that I was late because I was taking sleep tips from Would I Lie To You?.

FRIDAY 9 FEBRUARY 2024 (RUN)

A double day, a Daley Day, as I doubled up sports to both run and... play darts at a place called Flight Club. That's right: Flight Club. A perfect name for a darts club. Well, a secret darts club. Not so good a name for a darts club that advertises and relies on word of mouth. The first rule of Flight Club is tell your friends about Flight Club.

I've never played darts. I checked YouTube for videos on how to throw a dart. A man in a pub on screen explained how to stand, how to aim and how to keep the dart at 90 degrees so it flies straight and true. He didn't explain about gravity and how darts drop, and how hard it is to line up your hand to point at a spot on the board, or even, the basics of which hand to use. I'm left-handed but play golf and tennis with my right. What hand should I use?!?

I tried both and as the dart left my left hand it also left the board far behind and banged off the wall next to me. My right was right.

The other thing the video didn't say was that there is no way to handicap darts players. If someone is good, they will beat you as the one good player in our group showed again and again. "I've not played in 20 years," he said. "Aye," we said, "but you're 64, you could have been playing for the 44 years before that! We've only been playing four minutes!"

Overall, I don't think playing darts will have any training benefit to Celtman, not unless I get lost in the moor and need to construct a spear to hunt down a deer. If so, I will remember to throw with my right hand and not my left.

SATURDAY 10 FEBRUARY (BIKE)

The YouTube session. One hour of watching videos while keeping a steady pace. This time I watched reviews of a new Apple virtual reality headset.

Coincidently, yesterday, I tried a VR headset for the first time. A 12 year old son of a colleague had popped into the office and was waiting in a boardroom for their mum to finish. They'd brought a VR headset with them, so we all had a go.

I held lightsabres and slashed at flying boxes. It was a few minutes before I realised I could also move and duck, the immersion became more real as I forget about bumping into the real boardroom table as tried hard not to bump into the fake walls of the game. Something is wrong when you spend more time avoiding fake walls than real ones.

No such problems with virtual reality and riding indoors. Unless Apple also invent air conditioning then sticking a headset on your head will be no better than sticking trainers on your head. Ewwww.

SUNDAY 11 FEBRUARY 2024 (RUN)

Last time I ran the Kirkintilloch 12.5k it was the fifteenth anniversary of the race, though only the 14th time it had been held. That's what a global pandemic does to anniversaries – it makes years disappear. The race number was also confused. The numbers had "2020" printed on them. So, the 15th anniversary was the 14th race run under the banner of 2020 in 2022.

To make matters more confusing today for the 16th race on the 17th anniversary the original 12 hills had been replaced by 10 due to road works on part of the course.

Last time out, the problem with 12 hills was that you also have 12 'valleys' and those valleys quickly filled with puddles so deep they could have been French philosophers. The rain didn't stop for the entire race, the water flowed down every hill and it was difficult to avoid the thought that there must be better ways to spend a Sunday morning than running outside in Kirkintilloch: maybe diving into a pit of snakes or brushing your teeth with a Brillo pad or running a marathon while wearing a diving suit... all would be better options.

The other side to the rain was the cold that starts to seep through your body unless you keep your legs and arms pumping. All my fastest times in races have happened while it's been raining. I think rain makes you run faster. Usain Bolt may have run the fastest time ever for the 100 metres, but I bet you that Noah was a decent sprinter too when the rain started to fall.

No such worries today, a warmer than it appeared grey February morning. With changes to the course, it was an easier run than previous years and I felt good when I finished, especially as I didn't need to break into a front crawl just to get round.

MONDAY 12 FEBRUARY 2024 (REST)

Part of me wanted to ride again today to make up for Saturday's shorter ride. The rest of me wanted to do nothing and take the rest day after yesterday's race. I had a sausage roll for lunch and the answer was easy: rest day it was. Mmmmm, sausage roll.

TUESDAY 13 FEBRUARY 2024 (RUN)

After several weeks of training, I weighed myself this morning and I am .5kg heavier than I was when I started. That'll be the muscle, I thought. But my body fat had also increased so that'll be the sausage roll then.

I find it strange that the more I do the heavier I get, while at the same time my face is thinner than it was in December. I don't know anything about nutrition, so I don't know if I'm undereating, overeating or just having too much of a sweet tooth. I have a decent diet, most of my meals are made from scratch and I have a good variety of dinners. However, I do love chocolate and sugar and training is always an excuse to eat more. I've run a race, I can eat a cake. And a Mars Bar. And a bag of cookies. And a 1kg bag of Tate & Lyle. Over the next couple of weeks, I'll reduce the amount of sugar in my diet and will measure myself again.

WEDNESDAY 14 FEBRUARY 2024 (RUN)

Today is Valentine's day.

Roses are red.
Celtman t-shirts are blue.
I went for a run* because I want one too.

*even though it was bucketing, and I had to wear a waterproof jacket, and I got soaked by a bus when it hit a large puddle as I jogged on the pavement.

THURSDAY 15 FEBRARUY (SWIM)

"Congratulations," said Sean the coach, "you've come second in this race!"

Then he added: "There's only two of you racing but, still, you can tell your friends and family you were second in a race."

Also, last. I was last.

In this morning session we were split into pairs. As it's the school holidays, the pool was quiet and there were only four of us in the lane. That meant two pairs and 2x50m relay race.

I only have three swim speeds: float, swim and sink. This was new to me. I had to swim as fast as I could and beat the swimmer beside me. Except the swimmer was a woman, and I already knew she was slower than me as she always swam behind me in previous sessions. I thought it would be easy except I hadn't realized she has four speeds: float, swim, sink and swim fast. I lost easily. It wouldn't be fair to say I was second. I was third in a two-person race.

FRIDAY 16 FEBRUARY 2024 (REST)

Woke up with a head cold. Went to work with a head cold. Came home with a head cold. Decided that rather than try and fit a session on the bike in it would be better to take it easy and try and shake this off instead.

Instead, I check accommodation for Celtman.

I have slept in a living room, a cleaner's cupboard and what felt like a supermarket skip. Racing around the country is expensive and one of the skills all triathletes need is the ability to find the cheapest and closest accommodation to the start line as possible.

On Skye, Iain CeltBrother and I stayed in a hotel room whose window opened into a skip. Which was handy, as the room didn't have a bin. Or much in the way of sheets, paint, any Wi-Fi or hope of better days. Every hour someone would throw a glass in the skip. Every hour. All night.

In Dunkeld, I thought I'd found a bargain. £35 a night for a double room. The room was new. Recently renovated and had a smell which could only be described as Eau Du Crime Scene Clean Up Crew. My eyes started watering as soon as we opened the door. The smell of bleach was so strong, my teeth turned white. The room was so new I'm sure it was still a cleaner's cupboard that morning.

But not this time. This time we're staying at the Torridon, a luxury hotel only a few minutes from the finish line.

After years of slumming, I want something to look forward to at the end of the race.

Not that there's that much choice for Celtman. The Applecross peninsula is isolated and there's not a lot of accommodation. To make it harder, the peninsula forms part of the North Coast 500 tourist trail so any accommodation is already hard to find with tourists booking for their own tour of the Highlands.

So, no sooner were places confirmed than Iain scoured AirBnB and hotel websites for places to stay because there's no point having a place if you don't have a place to stay too. And not, thankfully, anywhere that will involve a rubbish dump, the eternal sun or more chemicals than the Rolling Stones dressing room.

If, however, you can't find somewhere to stay, don't panic. There's a Facebook forum for Celtman accommodation which contains tips and leads for accommodation with places appearing even days before the event. While 250 may have booked accommodation, between those dropping out and other tourists unable to make it, there will be plenty of opportunity for places.

SATURDAY 17 FEBRUARY 2024 (BIKE/SWIM)

When I wake it feels like I have two Footballs stuffed up my nose as I am so blocked up but by the time I'm up they're down to golf balls and I decide to try an hour on the bike. An easy workout follows, and I felt good afterwards. Later, I have a short swim after taking CeltChild to the pool. It always feels strange to swim with a cold, it makes me focus more on my nose as I breathe, even though I breathe through my mouth. I wonder if I had a broken leg, would I be thinking "how are my arms doing?" when I swam?

SUNDAY 18 FEBRUARY 2024 (BIKE)

Night Nurse should be called Night Tyson Fury for the speed it knocks me out. One cup before bed and I'm asleep faster than you can count to 10.

I wake up tired, but with my nose feeling normal. I was planning to ride first thing, but I decide to take it easy for most of the day before jumping on the bike before tea.

During the day, I look for a bike race to enter in late April or early May to give me a test of my endurance around 6 – 8 weeks before Celtman. I find one close to Glasgow, the Kinross Sportive, which has a 90 mile option. I think this would be a good test and book in.

I don't want to enter too many races before Celtman. Training is more important, but it's good to test both my legs and my bike in the run.

MONDAY 19 FEBRUARY 2024 (BIKE)

Monday is not a rest day, at least not this week. I wanted to get a long ride in as I've not had the chance to do that in the last two weeks after racing last weekend and being ill this weekend. Feeling better, I knew I had time today to get a few hours on the bike.

Before starting I chose to wear better fitted and padded cycle shorts, which worked for most of the ride but after two hours I was starting to wiggle on my seat to try and get a comfier position. I'm conscious that training can lead to injury but I'm hoping I won't have to go to see my GP for groin rash as there are many reasons for not starting a race, but groin rash is not one of them.

I've been injured. That's a common one: a strained ankle, shin splints or a dodgy knee. They're all common reasons for not starting. Less common is a broken rib caused by tying a bungee cord around my waist while playing five a side football aka Bungee Football.

Now, Bungee Football is a stupid, stupid game that recreates table football by tying players together with bungee cords so that they have to work together to play. Of course, it doesn't work like that because when you run right, the rest of your team runs left and you're thrown to the ground faster than a losing scratchcard. And, unlike an actual bungee, where a lot of time and effort is spent making sure that you don't hit the ground, in bungee football you hit the ground again and again and again until you break a rib.

I've never played it since.

But I did play it four days before I was meant to take part in the Caledonian Challenge, a 56 mile walk along the West Highland Way in 24 hours.

I tried to take part, I went up with my team the night before but, as I couldn't sleep as I couldn't lie on my chest and I couldn't carry a rucksack with tweaking my broken rib every time the chest strap moved across it, I had to pull out.

That wasn't the strangest reason I've ever had to pull out of a race. Iain CeltBrother and I were going to take part in the Tour of the Borders – a cycle Sportive starting in Peebles. The forecast was poor, it was meant to rain all day but we still went ahead as we knew we had waterproofs to manage the bad weather. It turned out though, that what we didn't have was a front window wiper for Iain CeltBrother's car. As we drove down, and as black clouds gathered and the forecast predicted the start of a 36 hour downpour, the windscreen wiper fell off Iain CeltBrother's car. Blimey!

We stopped at Abingdon Service Station to see if they had a replacement but they didn't have anything we could use. We were left with no choice: we could carry on, but with no wiper to clear the rain from the windows – and no certainty that if we could get to

Peebles before the rain started that we'd find a wiper there the next day so that we could drive home safely. Or, we could abandon the race and head home and order a wiper knowing we didn't have to drive again until it arrived. We decided to head home.

Most times though when I've abandoned a race it's because of the weather – I used to regularly take part in a half marathon in Fort William in November until I realised that of the five times I'd entered it, I'd only taken part twice. Fort William in November is a good month for submarines, goldfish and putting out fires. Every race day I'd open the curtains of my bed and breakfast, look out at the torrential rain and make a mental note to start gathering animals two by two.

When I think of Celtman 2020 now, I think of it in terms of the races I've not entered and how it compares. And I think it stands on its own as I can't think of another race where I'm injury free, the weather was good and I'd trained as much I could yet I couldn't take part. I blame Boris Johnson. And the virus. But mostly Boris.

However I don't regret not taking part because there was never a chance of taking part. Just like Bungee Football, there was a limit to how much I could do safely – and that limit was set by the pandemic. There was nothing I could have done to change it. And I'm just glad now that I hadn't pulled because of groin rash instead. That would have been embarrassing.

TUESDAY 20 FEBRUARY 2024 (SAUNA)

The world changed during the pandemic. Things we thought acceptable in 2019 were unacceptable in 2021. Things like shaking hands or picking pockets – it's the light-fingered larcenists who are the real victims of the coronavirus – or just generally being anywhere remotely near another human being. We needed to adjust to the 'new normal', a phase which instantly suggested life was worst. No one adds 'new' to a word without making you think you prefer the old one. New Coke? New Mutants? New York? All worse than old Coke, the original X-Men and an ugly cathedral that's easily flooded.

In this 'normal' (I'm not using 'new') there was one thing that we all did that seems even more abnormal then. Before lockdown, we would voluntarily sit in a wooden box and be sweated on by strangers. We called it a sauna, to make it sound more continental, we wore shorts, so as not to make it weird, but, when you break it down, a sauna nee sweatbox is nothing but a small room where strangers met up and dripped on each other.

Some saunas were weirder than others. The one in Stornoway was made of plastic so that it felt like you were a carrot in a steamer. To be accurate it was a steamer as it was a steam room rather than a sauna but room would suggest it was larger than a kettle pot while steam would suggest it wasn't a molten bast of heat that shot straight-out from underneath a single seat flaying any stray ankle that happened to be in its way. It wasn't an accident waiting to happen. It was an on-going disaster that required to be put out. It was Chernobyl in a sports centre.

In Glasgow, the Arlington Swimming Pool has a garden door as an entrance to its steam room. A proper white plastic fire door more commonly found in cheap extensions and infection control labs. The glass was so thick it could have a been a PE teacher. This room also featured a single furnace of heat to be avoided at all costs. But if it did hit you then you could cool off in the rivers of sweat that swept down the walls. The walls were so wet that Noah would have started building a second ark.

At my local gym the sauna is slightly more civilised. There is a pretend coal fire and you can ladle water from a bucket onto it to create steam. I don't bother though as I've seen the lifeguards collect the water by scooping it from the pool. Adding it to the fake fire doesn't create a nice steam effect, it turns the water into chlorine and the steam into mustard gas.

But the strangest thing I've ever seen in a sauna was a drug deal. Or at least I thought it was.

I was in a sauna with Mike Skinner of The Streets and his band. It was in a hotel in Glasgow and they must have been playing a show. One of the band started talking about the Dragon and how great it was in Leeds the previous night. I thought "Dragon, that's clearly drug slang for heroin – don't you chase the dragon?"

I thought I was going to get a tale of drugs and rock and roll until Mike Skinner said:

"The Dragon. Yes, lovely Chinese. I had the lemon chicken."

Today I still look at the sauna and think about what made us think that sitting in a room surrounded by the accumulated sweat of strangers and food critics was ever acceptable, or fun. Hot stuff? Hot zone, more like.

WEDNESDAY 21 FEBRUARY 2024 (RUN)

Prince Andrew doesn't sweat, and I believe him because I too don't sweat. At least not between October and April.

Don't get me wrong, I do sweat. I sat in a sauna yesterday and recreated the Victoria Falls. But, for six months of the year, it's difficult to sweat in Scotland because it's too cold. As soon as temperature drops, unless I've got more layers than a wedding cake, I can go out for a run and come back completely dry.

Sweating is meant to help cool you down. That's why we do it. It regulates our internal temperature, so we don't overheat. But, in Glasgow, in winter, there's no danger of that.

Instead, it would be so much easier if Charles Darwin was right, and evolution had helped Scottish athletes evolve into a cross between a runner and a Calor gas heaters. I don't need to sweat while running, I need to turn the gas up to avoid my hands turning blue and doing a good impression of the Na'vi of Avatar.

I know I can put on running tights, and gloves, a hat and a jacket. But that would just involve becoming half man half wardrobe. I want heat, not a catwalk.

I must admit though I do enjoy the days I can go running and not break a sweat as, when I get back, I can think "Do I really need a shower?" and skip it when I pass the sniff test.

You know the 'sniff test', don't you? Everyone does it. A quick sniff of the armpit and, if you smell nothing, then no shower is required.

(Never try this test with your feet, you'll never leave the shower).

April though is when the weather changes and sweating returns. It's as much a sign of Spring as new lambs, Easter eggs and forgetting your alarm clock automatically adjusts your clock and putting it forward an hour manually only to lose two hours (or is that just me?).

But even though sweating shows that temperatures are rising and the sun is shining, I do miss the winter months of being able to go for a run without having to shower as soon I get home.

THURSDAY 22 FEBRUARY 2024 (SWIM)

It's starting to get light as the session starts at 7am. Now, rather than stand in darkness waiting for the University of Strathclyde sport centre doors to open, we stand in half-light. Soon, it will be daylight and I might finally feel like I'm getting up at a sensible hour rather than at time that can only be shown on a clock between "too early".

Even though the alarm is only 20 minutes earlier than my normal alarm, it still feels like I've woken up the night before. After several weeks, I thought I would have adjusted to this start, but it still feels like I'm casing the house like a burglar when I try to get to the kitchen to have a silent breakfast without waking anyone.

FRIDAY 23 FEBRUARY 2024 (RUN)

Another tricky day to fit in a session. Mrs Celtwife is now in London and I have CeltChild to look after. The only time I had to train was the time to get to work in the morning. So, after the wee one had settled, I ran in and enjoyed one of my favourite types of run. The sunrise run where you start in twilight and finish in daylight. It may only have been a 30-minute run but it felt like I was running all night.

SATURDAY 24 FEBRUARY 2024 (BIKE)

It may be starting to get light but that doesn't mean it's starting to get dry. My original plan was to run into work this morning however I could tell it was raining without looking outside as our conservatory acts as a kettle drum whenever it rains. It amplifies every drop into a rimshot echoing around the house. If you want to know what it would be like to be trapped in a bongo, then come visit us when it rains.

It looks like it was going to rain all day, just as it has for most of January and February, but when I got home, thinking I would be riding indoors, the sun came out and I finally managed to get out.

Training in Scotland is mostly about checking the weather forecast.

SUNDAY 25 FEBRUARY 2024 (RUN)

A longer run and my body is now doing the strange thing of having strong legs but weak body. With running and cycling my legs are getting stronger but with less swimming, though still a longer swim each week, I can feel my body weaken before my legs as I run. It's a stranger feeling especially when the mind is weaker too after a harder week of training. I must keep telling myself that the running is easy, it's the standing upright that's hard.

MONDAY 26 FEBRUARY 2024 (REST)

How many times have you been asked to sponsor someone? Whether it's a marathon, a bungee jump or growing a moustache, we are asked all the time to give money for a good cause. In return, we promise to say "Well done!" when the race is over, the bungee rope holds or the moustache looks more like Henry Cavill in Mission Impossible than Henry the Hoover after vacuuming the hairs around a barber's chair. And that's it. Nothing else needed. Hand over cash, say congratulations. There's nothing else to do. Because why would you do anything else? It's a donation to charity. You don't expect to get if refunded, do you..?

Until a few years ago, I've never thought to check up on the sponsored person. I've never checked whether someone has ran around London or abandoned their razor. I just pay my money and I forget about it until I see an email saying "Thank you!"

Even if they don't complete the race, or even start, or if they remain bumfluff free for the next six months, I wouldn't never go back and ask for my money back. So why am I talking about it now? I'm talking about it because at the weekend I was reminded that when I raised money for driving from Plymouth to the Gambia, and the car broke down on day one – see the race diaries – someone asked for their sponsorship money back.

"I heard you crashed out," they said when I met them a few days after returning home.

"Well, we didn't crash," I said, "the engine just failed. There was nothing we could do. The car couldn't travel faster than 10mph. We could have kept going but we'd still be driving to Africa next year, if we stayed in the car. We had no choice but to quit."

"So you don't finish it?" They asked.

"No, we didn't finish it" I said.

"In that case, can I have my money back?"

They'd sponsored me £50. Or more accurately they'd sponsored Action for Children fifty pounds.

I thought they were joking so I said: "Would you like interest on that too?"

And they said, in the same tone they would speak to their bank manager: "no, the interest would be next to nothing. I only gave you the money two weeks ago. You can keep the interest."

"That's kind of you," I said but that's not what I was thinking, they genuinely wanted their money back.

"You can pay tomorrow," they said, "otherwise I will have to charge interest." And they weren't joking when they said that.

And I paid them because what other choice did I have? We had asked for sponsorship to reach Africa and we'd only spent one hour in France before the car broke down. They were quite right to ask for their money back. We'd been sponsored to travel, not sponsored to quit.

That's why it's important when receiving any sponsorship request to write back immediately with a list of conditions for your sponsorship. The first, of course, being that any money gifted is conditional of them completing the event. The second is that interest WILL APPLY if any refund is not paid within 48 hours. The third is that you know a man who will kick their door if they don't pay.

I guarantee these conditions will mean you will never lose money again when sponsoring someone – because you will never again be asked again to sponsor anyone. Except today, today I was asked to sponsor someone. It's another sign of Spring.

TUESDAY 27 FEBRUARY 2024 (BIKE)

Out of bed. Pull on shorts and t-shirt. Get on indoor bike. Start pedalling. Wake up after 10 minutes of cycling.

The best thing about cycling first thing is that you finish before you've even started the day. It feels like a rest day because you then have the rest of the day free. However, it can be a challenge to get up. To help, I set up the bike and put out my clothes the previous night. The only problem with this system is that it means I'm ready before I'm ready and it feels like I'm cycling while still trying to sleep.

I'm surprised no one has invented the bed bike yet. There are desk bikes. And bed bikes seem the next step. I'm not sure how the logistics of it would work. Maybe it should be more of a recumbent bike than a standard bike frame. You can lie back, pedal and pull the duvet firmly around you.

I'm onto a winner. Or maybe not because as soon as I wrote bed bike I thought I'd better Google it to see if someone had already invented it. And it turns out they have. The bed bike is used by patients in hospitals to help maintain muscle mass and blood circulation when bed bound. But maybe it can also be used for... extreme triathlon training?!

WEDNESDAY 28 FEBRUARY 2024 (RUN)

Today I thought about the first time I heard about Celtman.

"Mad," I'd said.

"Mental," agreed Iain CeltBrother.

But we carried on watching just the same.

The first time I saw Celtman was on Sunday 9 December 2012 when my brother and I watched The Adventure Show on BBC Two Scotland. Presenter Dougie Vipond explained how just over 100 people from around the world had, in June 2012, swam two miles, cycled 120 miles and then ran a marathon up and down a mountain. All we could say was "Why on earth would anyone do that?!?"

As Iain Celtbrother and I started to take part in triathlons, first a short mini-triathlon in Edinburgh (we came last), then longer events in Glasgow, Chester, Henley and Weymouth (all near the back of the race), our thoughts kept coming back to Celtman.

"Not that I'll ever do it," I said to my brother after we completed IRONMAN UK in 2015 – a 3.9km swim, a 112-mile cycle and a marathon that didn't involve a single mountain or even a slope. (But did involve us coming in near the end again.)

"I'll never do another race like that again," he answered.

"Not even Celtman?" I asked.

"No," he said, "I'm done.

"Me too," I said.

But neither of us meant it.

Over the next few years, we continued to race in Scotland and further abroad, but my thoughts always came back to Celtman. I'm from Stornoway in the Western Isles, and Celtman felt like home. It started in Sheildag, on the northwest coast of Scotland and it travelled along the western coast before descending the main road from Ullapool to Inverness, the only road connecting Stornoway with the mainland. If you look south and east from Stornoway, you can see the Celtman route. With powerful binoculars. And a bit of imagination. It felt so close.

But I'm not an athlete. I love to challenge myself but I'm happy to complete, not compete. I didn't have what it takes to take part in Celtman. It wasn't just a triathlon or a long-distance triathlon – it was an extreme triathlon.

The race starts with a two-mile swim in the cold waters of the west coast of Scotland. Even in Summer, the water temperature can be a single figure. I watched swimmers, strong swimmers, shaking uncontrollably at the end of the swim on that initial broadcast. Blue feet. Blue fingers. A perfect copy of James Cameron's Avatar. This wasn't just an extreme triathlon, it was out of this world.

The race continued with a circular bike ride from Sheildag to Kinlochewe, around 120 miles from what is now the North Coast 500 but which was then just the A832. Better branding may have helped sell the road to tourists in the 12 years since that initial race, but it hasn't reduced the hills or calmed the winds or stopped the rain.

From Kinlochewe the race headed off-road and uphill as competitors either climbed Beinn Eighe, a 3000m plus mountain with a narrow ridge separating split summits before a sharp gravelly descent or raced around Beinn Eighe, on a tough route along the gulley floor, before both routes finished in the small coastal village of Torridon.

"And it's completely unsupported," said Dougie Vipond. As if the race was not hard enough.

While most races have food and drinks supplied by organisers, Celtman has nothing. You can receive supplies from your own 'crew', who can drive around the route and join you on the run. But there is no one else to help. No marshal to help with repairs if you get a puncture, or volunteer to hand out water if you get thirsty. It's just you, the sea, the road, the mountain.

"And don't forget the jellyfish," said Dougie, almost sadistically.

The sea swim passes two islands in a bay. The islands, in Summer, provide the perfect spot for jellyfish to lurk.

"You will get stung."

But, even if I wanted to swim with jellyfish, there was no guarantee that wanting to take part would lead to a place. Ambition alone is not enough; you also need luck. To take part, you need to enter a ballot. There are only 250 places, and far more people want to take part than can compete. Instead, you enter the ballot and, if you're lucky, you can 'win' a place in the race. I can't think of any other competition – outside of the masochist's world championship - where the winner is hoping to suffer. But, if you are lucky enough to win this lottery instead of the actual lottery, then you count yourself among the small number of people who have a chance to take part in Celtman and who can, if successful, win either a blue or a white t-shirt.

It seems mean. Celtman is one of the toughest triathlons on the planet. Surely there must be a great prize at the end. But no, there is not. There is just a t-shirt. A blue T-shirt for those who climb Beinn Eighe and a white T-shirt for those who don't. There are no medals. No swag bag, and, sadly for someone delighted to find unlimited Domino's pizza at the end of IRONMAN UK, not even a biscuit to feast on at the finish line. It's just you and your inedible T-shirt.

THURSDAY 29 FEBRUARY (BIKE)

This year is a leap year which means there is an extra day in February.

Do you need to train on a leap day? It's an extra day. Can it be a rest day?

I decided to train. Hopefully everyone else rested and I'm now one day fitter than them!

CHAPTER 4

~~CELTMAN 2020~~ TODDMAN 2020

I blame Boris Johnson. The day after Boris announced a national lockdown the streets were filled with people out jogging, who had never jogged before. Either that or the streets were filled with Coronavirus sufferers as, everywhere I went, I saw people gasping, sweating and struggling to move.

I love that we spent years trying to get people to be more active, and it turned out the quickest way to do that was to order everyone to stay in their house. That's the British public for you. If you want to stop smoking, give everyone a pipe. I did worry that this upsurge in jogging would lead to its own problems. After two weeks of running, it wasn't a Coronavirus wave we faced it was a pandemic of shin splints.

At the time, I was happy to work at home. I used the time gained in not commuting 90 minutes each day to help with training for Celtman instead. And, to keep things local, I trained by running to every street on a page of a Glasgow A-Z map which included my house. This was an area approximately two miles by two miles and which I thought would take me a month to complete. How wrong I was. After 50 runs, averaging six miles each time, I finally completed the page. To put it in context: there were nearly 200 pages in my street map (though it does cover half of Ayrshire and the Central Belt), which meant I completed 0.5% of central Scotland...

I really should have got a street map with a smaller area. My progress would have been more impressive - in the same way an advert for a sofa always makes the cushions seem bigger by hiring very small models to sit on them   I ran a postcode rather than a page of an entire city map.

This was not the only lesson I learned. I had some simple rules I followed. The first was that I would always start from the house. No cheating by driving to a new part of the map to run. If I wanted to run a street two miles away, I had to run four miles to get there and back.

There was a purity in running every street from my home. It's what the Pope would do, as he's very pure. Although I have to point out that he would have a much easier task. The Vatican state is very small. He could run every street just by crossing St Peter's Square. However, if you're not the Pope, and I'm confident the Pontiff is not be reading this, then you'll probably have quite a few streets to run. And while the first ten or so runs will spiral out from your home, the next runs will involve you having to run along the streets you've previously claimed to get to your new world of virgin streets. After a few more runs, you'll find you're running 1 – 2 miles to get to the new streets and suddenly your average run has risen from 4 – 6 miles to 6 – 9 miles because you feel that you at least need to make a good effort to claim the streets after you get there.

So, just like the Pope, I feel I need to absolve you of your sins. Once you get to that stage, if I was doing this again, I'd say it's okay to drive a bit or cycle over before starting. I didn't. But I am pretending to be the Pope in this example so must be whiter than white. However, in future, now that I've finished my page, I will have no hesitation in driving from my house to get to a 'start line'.

The second rule I had was no maps. You may feel tempted to look at your phone to check where you are or what streets you need to cover. And for this, I must confess, that I did sin. For yea, didst I look upon the Google Maps whilst trying to find a street that I'd missed the first time and didn't want to miss a second time as I'd already ran two miles to get there. But, if you can, try not to use your phone. There is nothing more satisfying than working out the layout of a new housing estate just by looking at the road and checking whether it's covered in tarmac like a public road (which is likely to have roads branching from it) or is made of bricks like a private drive (and likely a dead end).

And, you know what else? Orienteers use maps. And no one wants to be an orienteer. Orienteering is nothing but geography with trainers. Who knows what an ox-bow lake is? Geographers. Who know how to run to an ox-bow lake? Orienteers, that's who. Dweebs. Avoid.

Most of all, after running all these streets I found a new love of the area I live – because these were no longer Glasgow's streets, they were my streets. I was an explorer conquering streets and planting my flag on Dirleton Drive, Tantallon Road and Pollockshaws Road. Maybe one day, they would name these streets after me?

But just as running every street took longer than I thought, so lockdown continued longer and longer without any sign of it easing.

"We'll be home for two weeks," I had thought at first, then life will go back to normal. But as we all know, those weeks turned into months, and those months turned into a massive conspiracy theory where Bill Gates planted microchips into our brains as we slept. Did the virus happen or was it all a Matrix like simulation?!?

Either way, as I finished running the streets around my home, Celtman was cancelled as social distancing meant that it would have been reckless to have 250 triathletes and their supporters descend *en masse* on a small town in the Highlands, even if those triathletes were going to spend 16 hours swimming, cycling and running and being almost as socially isolated as you can be while not being on the moon.

Instead of Celtman, and to comply with both the letter and the spirit of social distancing laws and regulations, Iain CeltBrother and I created our own race, using Iain's house as a transition. We could start at a reservoir, cycle from it using public roads to Iain's house, then run back over moor and a hill, Meikle Bin, to get back to the start. The finish line would be the car park at the base of Meikle Bin and, just like the infamous Berkely Marathon, the winner would be the first to touch a gate.

To make it Covid compliant, as I was travelling to another

household, the event could only take place with people called Todd who were related to each other. So, instead of Celtman we had the inaugural Toddman Extreme Triathlon.

While lockdown wasn't a time for winners and losers, everyone was a winner no matter what they did during that endless lockdown. It's also right to say that the history books did record an actual winner. Me.

It was close. If you've ever read or watched documentaries about the legendary 'Iron War' between Dave Scott and Mark Allan as they battled to become the IronMan world champion in 1989 then you will know what ToddMan was like, toe to toe. Neither competitor more than 2 metres apart for the whole race. A race for the ages.

Iain CeltBrother and I were side by side (a socially distanced two metres apart) for the whole race - except for final 20 meters when I saw the car park and sprinted to the finish line and Iain saw the car park and stopped and said "car park" and forgot to run.

Winners act, losers state the bleedin' obvious.

Now, I know that there was some controversy to my finish. The winner had to touch a gate to finish. However no one said which gate. And there were two gates at the car park. And while I touched 'a gate', Iain claimed it was not 'the gate' he meant when he came up with the finish line. But, just as Iain said "car park" instead of running, he also said "gate" without naming which one to touch. So, I called dibs on the gate and claimed my title: Toddman champion 2020.

And, after the disappointment of Celtman's cancellation, I was proud to say that while I didn't travel to the Highlands, I at least had my title and I'd completed my ambition of getting to the bottom of page 97 of the Glasgow A to Z.

CHAPTER 5

MARCH 2024

FRIDAY 1 MARCH 2024 (REST)

How many sports are too many sports? Some people take part in just one sport. Some might try two and take part in a duathlon. Others will take part in three and enter a triathlon. After that, you're in the realm of pentathlons, heptathlons and decathlons. But once you get more than three, you may get a few hours or even an overnight rest between events. Was Olympic gold medal winning heptathlete Jessica Ennis a true multi-sport athlete? She did complete in eight events to win gold. But she also got to sleep between events. Does a multi-sport event need to be continuous?

And does a heptathlon have seven events or does it have six? You run both the 200m and the 800m. In duathlons you also run twice (along with a bike ride) and it only counts as two events. If you repeat an event, even at a different distance, is it not the same event?

I ask this because Hyrox, a multi-event fitness race, has either 16 events or nine. There are eight 1km runs between eight other events. Does each run count as a separate event or is it just one? Is Hyrox a novathlon (9 events) or a something-in-Latin-for 16-athlon? I'm going with novathlon, just 'cause it sounds cooler, and is easier to pronounce.

Tomorrow, I'm taking part in a Hyrox event in Glasgow and I'm taking part in the same way that Jessica Ennis takes part in the heptathlon. I'm taking the evening off and having a rest.

SATURDAY 2 MARCH 2024 (NOVATHLON)

Hyrox. The first run was straightforward. It was two laps of an indoor hall at Glasgow's SECC. The route was marked with fast and slow lanes to help separate people. But it didn't really matter as there was plenty of room to run at my own pace. The fact there were two laps gave plenty of opportunities for spectators to watch. And, at this point, admire my fast and sleek running style.

The first event was a 1km ski challenge (on Concept2 SkiErg machine). Each event was marked in the hall with a large easy to spot number so it was easy to find where to go. The machines were set at '6' but you can change this as long as you do it before you start and not halfway through. I'd never used a SkiErg before so, rather than practice, I watched a YouTube video and tried to remember what it showed about how to use the machine.

Back out and another 1km run. I realised there was a large screen showing the names of everyone on the track. The screen helpfully tells you whether you're on lap 1 or 2 and what event you're doing next, which in my case was the 50m Sled Push (150kg)

I was dreading this one. I had no idea whether I could push 150kg. I hadn't practiced (which you can take as read now for all the other events) and had only watched a video to see the technique required. This was a struggle. Back out on the run with rubbery legs before the 50m Sled Pull (120kg).

I didn't watch a video for this one. Whoops. You have a rope to pull and a small white square marked on the ground to stand in. I thought you couldn't move in the square so struggled to pull the sled without moving my feet. I was leaning back to try and use my weight to help but it was a tough challenge to complete the first 12.5m pull until Iain CeltBrother, who was in the next lane, told me I could move my feet. After that it was a lot easier to pull as I could walk backwards in the square before another run, more jelly legs then - what the blimey! - I have never burpeed (is this a word?) before. Again, I saw it on a video and thought it looked easy. How wrong I was. The next event was 80m of burpee jumps. You have to lie on the ground, stand back up. Jump. Repeat. If felt like I wasn't moving at all. Every time I lay down, I didn't want to get back up.

Awful. Though one of the judges said "nice technique" which was good to hear especially as Iain CeltBrother was sent back twice for getting it wrong. What a berk-ee!

And then, hallelujah, back on the run and I'm not burpee-ing (is this also a word?) as we come back in for the 1km Row (on Concept2 Rower). And, for the first time, I've used a rowing machine before and a 1km row was straightforward. This was the closest I got to a rest before two more runs and two more events, both strength based. The first was 200m Kettle Bells Farmers Carry (24kg). This was tough on the shoulders but not too bad. The main thing here was to make sure to use lots of chalk on my hands to stop any sweat on the handles as any sweat makes the kettle bells harder to carry. While the second event was 100m Sandbag Lunges (12kg) which destroyed my legs with alternate lunges while carrying a sandbag. Again, not a difficult task once I got into a rhythm, but I did feel it when I started the final run. Legs gubbed before I faced the final misery of throwing a ball against a high target 100 plus times in the 100 reps wall balls (6kg) challenge.

I've added 'plus' because if you don't hit the target then the throw doesn't count. I found this out as I was keeping track of the numbers along with a spotter/judge (who has a number clicker to keep track) and I counted 20 and he had 18. By the time I was at 90 he was at 80 and I'm sure I threw the ball 110 times before he said I'd completed the 100.

This was a tough end to the race. The 100 balls seemed to go on forever and I only got through this one as Iain CeltBrother said "remember to ask for the box" when we entered the station. The box is a handy seat that you sit on before standing and throwing. The box ensured that I squatted correctly. You can squat without the box but why would you give up a handy seat to rest on too!?

About halfway through, my spotter said "you're 10 ahead of your brother, you're not going to let him win, are you?". I wasn't and I made sure to keep ahead of him so I could be first to the finish line. A proper ramp to run up. Loud music. A congratulations and a banana. What more do you need for a finish?

I enjoyed this one. The variety keeps it entertaining. The venue is big enough to ensure there's no bunching on either the run or at any of the stations, and small enough to make it easy for spectators to keep up with the action. But my legs make jelly look like concrete and my shoulders are more wound up than a TalkSport phone-in. In the words of R.E.M: everything hurts. But at least I have my dignity as here's the thing about Hyrox. It seems to remove most male seen of decency as half the competitors raced topless. Why did they race topless? I have no idea. You spend part of the event with your chest on the ground doing burpees, why you would to be naked on the same spot everyone else has sweated on is something I don't understand. Are they more aerodynamic? Is it a macho thing? Did they just forget their gym kit, and, like a Primary School PE class, they were made to take part anyway? I have no idea. But if you do decide to take part, please remember your t-shirt. If not me, at least for Mrs Celtwife, who dammed the confidence of all of them by loudly saying "It's not like they're even braw."

SUNDAY – TUESDAY 3 – 5 MARCH 2024 (REST)

If training is all about consistent improvement than Hyrox is a terrible event to include in a training programme. It targets your arms, back and shoulders and could help with the swim but the only thing you're swimming in is the sweat from the other half naked competitors. You use muscles you have never used before and that meant your legs will be gubbed and even bending over was painful and stiff. While, on Tuesday, my forearms became numb and stiff too. I couldn't work out at first why they were sore when they were fine on Sunday and Monday. It took me a couple of hours to realise that both forearms were sore in the same place. And, as such, it was likely to be bruising from catching the 6kg wall ball 100 times in my arms. Hyrox: the sport that keeps on giving you... internal injuries.

WEDNESDAY 6 MARCH 2024 (REST AND SAUNA)

If you're familiar with the name Bikram, it probably conjures up images of yoga, Netflix documentaries, or a rather disturbing combination of both. He's the famous yoga guru who pioneered the practice of hot yoga, and the infamous yoga guru accused of using his power to abuse and exploit women. The Netflix doc 'Bikram: Yogi, Guru, Predator' delves into all the allegations.

For me, though, the name Bikram triggers one specific memory: sweaty underpants.

Let me explain. I once attended a Bikram hot yoga studio. With the room cranked to a sweltering forty degrees, most men opt for shorts. Not the guy in front of me. He sported a pair of off-white y-fronts that, with each bend and stretch, offered a translucent (and utterly unwelcome) view of his backside. Worse, escape was impossible.

"No one leaves," the instructor announced, locking the door. "If you're hot, just drink some water. Leaving is cheating!"

Not helpful, considering my view.

You might think that's the worst hot yoga experience imaginable, but you'd be wrong. The early days of hot yoga in Glasgow involved a DIY enthusiast who transformed his flat into an unregulated, fire-hazard of a 'studio'. Think towels crammed around windows, gas fires blazing, and enough sweat to rival the Amazon rainforest... in a tenement building.

Our instructor would periodically interrupt the poses: "Anyone fancy a Greggs sausage roll? Or is it just me?" We'd be mid-asana, and he'd be daydreaming about lunch.

Thankfully, the tenement sauna days are gone. The practice moved to a proper West End studio... right next to a Greggs bakery, ironically enough. Though the old studio was warm enough to bake a Chicken lattice.

Sadly, the studio is closed, perhaps a victim of lockdown. I still smile whenever I pass by, as I did today, imagining the instructor finally able to indulging in his mid-class cravings by popping out for a Greggs halfway through a sun salutation.

THURSDAY 7 MARCH 2024 (BIKE)

Can I put my socks on without gritting my teeth and bracing myself for pain? Yes. Damn. That meant today I had to start training again. To break myself back in: a long but gentle spin on the bike.

FRIDAY 8 MARCH 2024 (BIKE)

And again. Easy does it.

SATURDAY 9 MARCH 2024 (REST)

Not easy enough. Felt knackered and decided another rest day was needed before getting back into a routine. Also, I wanted to watch Dune 2 at my local cinema and, as it's over two and half hours long, I was struggling to find the time to fit in some training and to go to the cinema to see it.

As I miss another day, I realised that only looking at my training a week ahead at a time has a fatal flow. I'd not thought about training for Hyrox so went from a decent block of training straight into an event I was completely unprepared for. I should have included some rowing and weightlifting in the weeks before to get better adjusted to taking part. Instead, I've been thrown off my training and had an inconclusive week while arms and legs recovered from their unexpected trials.

SUNDAY 10 MARCH (BIKE)

Start again. Back on the bike.

MONDAY 11 MARCH 2024 (SWIM)

Start again. Back in the pool

TUESDAY 12 MARCH 2024 (RUN)

Start again. Back on the streets. And another race coming up this week. Did I not just learn my lesson from Hyrox? Look ahead. Train for the race. Instead, a couple of months ago, I entered a half marathon this Sunday in Alloa and then forgot all about it.

I've raced here twice before even though I've never wanted to run it. Two reasons: there's a five mile long straight and, well that's it, there's a five mile long straight! Who want to run in a straight line for five miles?

(I realise I have also said a few weeks back: "who wants to run in a circle?" so maybe I should just say "who wants to run?!?").

There is an alternative. I love 'drunk running', the kind that doesn't involve any straight lines. I love 'scary movie running', the kind that promises a surprise around every corner. I don't want to see where I'm going for the next half an hour as I move forward in a long line of other people all going in the same direction. That's not running, that's high energy queueing.

Despite this, it's a very popular race with nearly 3,000 runners. We had to queue to get into Alloa. And it's not a high energy queue, we had to queue bumper to bumper as runners tried to get to the start on time. It was the same story on the way out. Not that it's a surprise that people would queue to get out of Alloa. It's the kind of town that inspires people rush to the exit.

WEDNESDAY 13 MARCH 2024 (REST)

I knew before starting this training that I would be racing for the white t-shirt. I'm not an athlete and I know my limits. For Celtman, to 'win' the blue t-shirt, you need to reach a checkpoint at the base of Beinn Eighe within 11 hours and 30 minutes. To 'win' the white T-shirt, you need to reach the checkpoint within 13 hours and 30 minutes. I knew before I started that I couldn't ride and run fast enough to make the first checkpoint. While I could get faster with training, I also knew that I wouldn't have time to train to do so as I had a young child and family commitments that meant my training would be limited. I could though, with the time I had and with smart training, safely make the cut-off for the white t-shirt. Or at least that's what I hope.

This diary is an attempt to show what it's like for an average triathlete to take on Celtman and to try and fulfil a dream that was sparked by that first broadcast on the BBC in 2012. I realised today that while I have recorded my thoughts each day, I've not recorded my actual training plan. I thought about sharing it, but my goal may not be your goal and what you want to do and what you enjoy will be very different from mine. While I'm not the fastest triathlete on the planet, I am the fastest Andrew Todd from Stornoway on the planet. And I'm an expert in what Andrew Todd from Stornoway can do and how to motivate him to train. For Coach Todd, I know that Athlete Andrew can complete a long-distance swim with only a minimum amount of swimming. But Coach Todd also knows that Athlete Andrew can only run longer distances if he's running consistently. Therefore, Coach Todd's training reflects Athlete Andrew's goal for the race of comfortably making the cut-off time for the white t-shirt while also making sure he runs, bikes and swims in a way that works for him. Saying that I did start with an actual training plan, but, as you've read, I've not mentioned it in a few weeks and I soon ditched it. It turns out Athlete Andrew didn't like being told what to do.

However, in sharing my training I do hope that it can inspire you to believe that a challenge like Celtman is possible, even for those of us usually found on the last page of race results. I'm a great believer in finding inspiration from other people and I think it's universal that we are inspired by the people around us. It's said that when Roger Bannister became the first man to run a mile in under four minutes, within a month his time had been beaten twice by two different athletes. It just takes the inspiration of knowing someone else has done something for the extraordinary to become ordinary.

Not that my tale is extraordinary. It's the opposite, it's insufficiently ordinary. It's sub-ordinary. It's the tale of a man getting on a bike in his spare room 3 – 4 times a week for six months, it's a tale of a man who runs 2 – 3 times a week and who, despite all proper coaching saying otherwise, only swims once a week. It's a story of repetition. It's a story of persistence. It's a story anyone can do if they just set their alarm a little earlier each morning and get up and do something before their waking brain tells them "Wait. What are you doing? Stay in bed!". Because training for a race like Celtman or for any challenge that you've not attempted before is nothing if not persistence.

THURSDAY 14 MARCH 2024 (SWIM)

It's light when I get up at 610am to get to the swimming pool. It makes a difference. It no longer feels like the middle of the night when I get up. Now, it just feels like the end of the night. A subtle difference but one that makes it slightly more bearable to be up and about before the house wakes up.

FRIDAY 15 MARCH 2024 (RUN)

The best thing about running in March is that running after work is just the right time to be running during the golden hour when the sun is low in the sky, and everything has a golden glow. It's one of my favourite times to run as, if you time it just right, you can start in the golden hour, run through the blue hour, after the sun sets, and finish in darkness. It makes it feel like you've run all day, even though it's only a short time around sunset.

SATURDAY 16 MARCH 2024 (SWIM)

I should be on the bike but with the race tomorrow I decide a swim was the better option to keep my legs fresh. Next week though: back to the long bike rides.

SUNDAY 17 MARCH 2024 (RUN)

If you'd asked me when was the last time I'd ran the Alloa Half Marathon I would have guessed 2019, the year before lockdown. In fact, it was seven years ago in 2017.

I blame lockdown. After two years of the pandemic, my sense of time is screwy. I discount the two years spent at home and assume everything is two years shorter than it is, which is why I'm planning to celebrate my twenty first birthday this year...

The one thing I remembered about the race was the bad traffic queue into Alloa before the race but when I phoned Iain CeltBrother to say we should arrive early, he disagreed. The start line had moved from near the town centre to a community campus on the edge of town. He didn't think the traffic would be as bad as there was a lot more routes to get to the start, including buses from the town centre for those who wanted to park further away.

He was right. It was easy to drive in, find a bus and get to the start. The only queue this year was at the pre-start toilets. But there's always a queue at the toilets before any race and it's always the case that no matter when you join that queue, whether one hour or five minutes before the start, and no matter how many people are in the queue, ten or a hundred, you'll never reach the front until two mins before the race starts and you'll come out to find everyone has already left. Alloa was no different. And we joined the race about two minutes after the start gun was fired. However, as there were over 1500 taking part, there were still waves crossing the line when we joined.

Overall, it was a cracking day for a race. A light cooling breeze and the changes to the route has improved the whole experience. I was pleased with a time of 1 hour 42 mins, which was faster than my previous time of 1 hours 48 mins and shows that while lockdown may have lost two years, I've gained six minutes.

MONDAY 19 MARCH 2024 (REST)

At the end of the Alloa Half Marathon, as I watched the finish line for Iain CeltBrother to arrive, a male runner in a black t-shirt, fell to the ground. He tried to get back up. However as he struggled onto his knees, the strength left his legs and he fell again. He looked exhausted, dazed and ready to give up. Two men jumped the barriers and grabbed him under the arms and hauled him up. They tried to walk him along the final 20m to the finish line, but his feet wouldn't move, his legs gave way and he fell back to the ground. A medic then jumped the barrier and ran over to help and all I could think was:

"If I collapse, I want everyone to know that I don't want to get to the finish line, I want a medically trained professional to check me out fist. CPR first, medal second. That's my philosophy."

There should be a box to tick on medical forms for races that tells organisers that you don't want to be a hero or a star of an inspirational TikTok video. You just want a check-up and all clear. Times don't matter, you can finish later. Just give me a couple of aspirin and a banana for sustenance.

I appreciate the spectators were doing the guy a favour. They must have thought he needed help to complete the race. But if you need help to complete a race, you also need help to see a doctor and priorities suggest medic first, podium second.

I suspect he was running too fast as he wanted to be first to get to the toilet. There's over 1500 runners at Alloa but, as far as we could see, there were only 10 Portaloos for everyone, which is not nearly enough. That's why I think he was running to try and avoid the queue at the end.

TUESDAY 19 MARCH 2024 (BIKE)

I was looking for a comment I wrote on a Facebook page for the Glasgow Triathlon Club when I found a note I wrote after IronMan UK in 2015.

"Swam a bit. Rode a bit. Ran a bit. Walked a lot. Happy to finish. Will never do it again.

"I just wanted to share six AMAZING tips I learnt from the race that you won't find in Don Fink's training guide*.

"Tip 1: Crash at least once when it's totally not your fault. I did and I promise that you'll forget about your legs as you spend the next 20 miles daydreaming about a bike pump, the rider who crashed into you and the elaborate torture porn of the Saw films.

"Tip 2: Your nose will run. It will never stop. Why not devise your own word for wiping your nose on your sleeve, arm, shoulder, any dry patch of jersey really. Snotting anyone?

"Tip 3: You can leave a special needs bag to pick up during the bike course. You could leave spare gels and energy bars or, you could do what I did, and leave a cheese & ham sandwich and a packet of crisps. It may take a couple of minutes to stop and eat it but, after a constant diet of gels, bars and electrolyte drinks those few minutes were the highlight of my day. Mmmm.... Cheesy Wotsits!

"Tip 4: We all run our own races. That's true. But, secretly, in our heart of hearts, we all get a boost when we see a fat bloke struggle. (This is an equal opportunities tip – remember, for the people ahead of you, you will be their 'fat bloke').

"Tip 5: Spectators will cheer you. They'll shout, "You're doing great", "Keep going", "You're running really well" etc, etc. However, sometimes, you know you're not doing great. You're walking. You're crawling. You've given up and had a cry at the side of the road. At those times, the spectators should shout "You're crap", "You'll never make it", "The fat bloke's beating you". Sometimes we need a bit of humiliation and tough love from strangers. For your next Ironman, to run faster, why not wear a gimp mask?

"Tip 6: Finally, a tip I've never read before. This must be a special tip reserved only for the most dedicated Ironmen and women. I call it "Recycling". It works like this: at some point during the race, you'll need to go to the toilet. When you do – why not eat a banana? You're hands are free. You've got time. You're not going anywhere. So why not put in what you're… erm… putting out?

"I've no other explanation for the amount of food found in the portaloos: folk are chewing and pooing – and they're heading to Kouna! This could be you (but, please God, wash your hands, you're an athlete, not an animal!).

"*tips not found in Don Fink's book for good reason!"

Reading it back I was also reminded of another tip I meant to share after the Alloa Half Marathon: if you are a spectator, always spell check your sign. There is a big difference between "Come on Derek" and other more pornographic spellings. Derek, I can only assume, was not looking for that level of support in Alloa.

WEDNESDAY 20 MARCH 2024 (SWIM)

A few months ago, Glasgow City Council extended the expensive city centre parking charges to cover the streets around my swimming pool. Instead of a pound to park, it was now over £5. However, I read online that if you didn't pay then the chances of a parking notice were so small you would save money paying an occasional fine than paying to park. Tonight, I can confirm that I am now £10 richer. After parking seven times, I was finally fined £30 for not having a parking ticket. Now I wonder what other 'crimes' I can commit to save money. Will I get a knock on the door if I don't pay my TV licence? How seriously do council's chase council tax? If I rob a bank, will the police look for me? Where is the

Martin Lewis of crime when you need him?

THURSDAY 21 MARCH 2024 (BIKE)

An early start as my wife was catching the plane to London. So early in fact, that I was finished, showered, had my breakfast, and woke up the wee one before 8 o clock. By the time I came home at night it felt so long ago that I thought I should get another ride in. I didn't. I'm not daft. But I did think about it. Let this be a warning to you: if you train too early in the day you may not realise you have trained at all.

FRIDAY 22 MARCH 2024 (REST)

I meant to run at lunchtime. I'd even brought my kit to the office. But a pre-lunch meeting ran over and that was the only thing than ran today as I didn't have time after work to catch up.

SATURDAY 23 MARCH 2024 (BIKE)

A split session. One hour in the morning then breakfast and family time before a longer ride later after I had the house to myself.

During the longer ride, I planned to have an energy gel halfway through. I was trying a new one as I'm running out of my favourite gels as the manufacturer, I love doesn't make gels anymore. I received my last box a couple of months ago and I'll have used them all by the time Celtman starts. I need to find a new gel.

For some that would be easy, but I really loved that gel.

When out riding, some people have a favourite cake stop or coffee stop or, for the hardcore and borderline alcoholics, a favourite pub stop, but, for me, I have a favourite bin stop.

I don't like carrying the remains of energy gels around in my back pocket because the pocket just fills with leftover gels until it feels like diving into high sugar swamp every time you reach in for another. Uggh.

That's why I have a bin stop. Somewhere I can stop and have a gel and immediately throw it into a bin. My soggy pocket problems are solved.

My favourite bin stop is at Whitelee Windfarm, near Eaglesham. It's the highest point of one of my usual routes and a good point to stop and have a gel before carrying on.

Normally, I wouldn't tell anyone that I had a favourite bin stop for the same reason I wouldn't tell you my preferred technique to cut my toenails, how I clean my ears or the satisfaction I might get from a pick of my nose. There are some things you just keep to yourself – and not even your nearest and dearest know that the real reason you're smiling is that you managed to extract an entire bogey in one go with just a deft flick of an expertly judged fingernail.

But my last ride to the bin stop was also the day I got the bad news that my gels were being discontinued.

What do I do now? I've used the same gels for 10 years. I have one halfway through a bike ride. I have a gel after swimming. I have a gel after 5 miles while running. If I had any more gels, I'd turn into one. Which would be doubly tragic as I'd probably eat myself because I was so tasty.

Instead, I'll need to find a new gel that I can eat and eat and eat and know that it won't be too sweet or too sour or too thin or too thick or to chalky or to smooth. Where do I turn now?

So, while taking part in my weekend long ride, I'm also trying different flavours and types of gels. Road testing, if you will. But without an actual road.

SUNDAY 24 MARCH 2024 (RUN)

Before my run, a box of gels arrives. And they came with a message on the front of the box. An unexpected message. It said, "Carefully packed by Sam" and it has a headshot of an attractive blonde woman.

Now, while I'm all for manufacturers telling you that they take care packing their products, they shouldn't *actually* need to tell you that. It should be a basic requirement of delivering anything that you didn't throw it into a box higgledy piggledy before mashing it down, throwing it as hard as you could against a brick wall before stamping on it to make sure the lids closes. That's Royal Mail's job. The manufacturer should be sending everything packed carefully.

However, it was nice that they'd taken the time to highlight this as an important step. Unnecessary, but nice.

But what I do have issue with, what I really don't believe, is that "Sam" had anything to do with it.

Maybe, I'm wrong. Maybe their warehouse is filled with good looking women taking an almost unhealthy interest in packing energy gels boxes in brown delivery boxes to middle aged men on bikes. Maybe she placed this sticker here with her own fair hand, a fair hand shared with the hundred other beautiful women of the shop floor all desperate to provide MAMIL's with much needed banana tasting energy boosts.

Perhaps the gel manufacturer is at the cutting edge of female empowerment in the warehouse packing industry. Maybe they sponsor deprived woman from inner city communities, train them and teach them and school them in the ways of packing boxes.

Or perhaps Sam is a lone trailblazer in a male dominated industry where to handle a package you need to, well, be able to handle your own package.

Maybe Sam is the Emily Pankhurst of box packers? Maybe she's a feminist icon in waiting? Maybe just maybe Sam is real.

Or maybe, almost certainly, it was packed by Dave from Rotherham.

Dave who farts on the boxes and scratches his bum.

That Dave.

Not Sam.

Dave.

I hate you, Dave.

You lied to me, Sam.

And you didn't even pack it carefully – a corner was squashed.

MONDAY 25 MARCH 2024 (RUN)

Monday is not a rest day this week as I'm working in Elgin, one of my favourite places to run.

I was running through Cooper Park in Elgin tonight when I passed the library and a bunch of teenagers hanging out on its steps. Which was good to see. Teenagers hanging out at the library. They must be the cool kids, I thought. Probably exchanging thoughts on whether 'the Blah Book' by Nigel Tomms really does challenge the stifling formality of language by writing a one million word long sentence where every second word has been replaced by the word "Blah" or whether it challenges anyone not to laugh at such pretentious twaddle as books are meant to, as a minimum, be, you know, read and understood.

And then one boy turned to the other and said: "Gonna give us a poond".

"Wha fir?" said the other.

"It's a poond an eccie and ahm gonna get wasted!"

Which made me think. How can an eccie, which I assume is an ecstasy tablet, not being up with the old drug lingo, be a pound? How can it be cheaper than a legal drug like alcohol or cigarette? Has the market fallen out of eccies. Is there a big warehouse with a secret stash of unsold tablets somewhere in the Moray countryside where the local drug dealer has no choice but to have a fire sale before the spring/summer eccies arrive?

Or was the kid being conned? Was someone selling Smarties and pretending they will get you high?

Or are drugs just really cheap?

They don't tell you that in school.

"Don't take drugs!" Says the teacher.

"Why not!" We say.

"They're too cheap! Save up and get a proper drink like a Buckfast – like a real man!"

When I got back, I Googled "How much do drugs cost" and I was surprised to learn how cheap heroin is too.

Then I checked the price of new energy gels.

And, having checked the price of energy gels and energy bars and comparing them against the latest street prices I can confirm that I will be running Celtman on a nutrition plan of one ecstasy every hour and a shot of heroin at the end of each stage. It's the economic choice. I'd be daft if I didn't try and save money by buying my 'nutrition' on the black market. Triathlons can be expensive, but not if you shop around.

TUESDAY 26 MARCH 2024 (REST)

No time for training. Back down the road from Elgin.

WEDNESDAY 27 MARCH 2024 (BIKE)

I'm now riding so long that my iPad can't keep up. It ran out of power before I could finish.

Which goes to show the amount of training I'm doing, or it confirms that I forgot to charge it before starting. I like to think it was the first option.

THURSDAY 28 MARCH 2024 (SWIM)

Swim before work, sauna after work, and all I could see was another man's knackers.

It was difficult to avoid them. They were staring me in the face. It was surprising to see them because, well, I was sitting in the middle of a sauna that was, crucially:

A. Open to men and woman; and

B. Not a nudist beach.

"Hello," said the knackers. Or the man. It was difficult to know where to look. Knackers or man. Man or knackers.

"Hello," I said, wondering if I should say something like "PUT SOME CLOTHES ON!"

"It's nice here," he said.

"It is," I said, again wondering if I should say something like "PUT SOME CLOTHES ON NOW!!!"

"I've never been here before," he said.

Clearly not.

He then sat up.

I should mention that throughout this entire conversation he'd been lying down, stretched out on his back on a raised wooden bench that encircled the sauna, while I'd just sat down on a lower bench and had turned my head and gazed straight into his knackers.

Sitting up didn't improve anything. Now everything dangled.

And still he acted like it was perfectly normal to be sitting in the nude in the middle of a sauna, open to all.

And still I didn't tell him to put some clothes on because, well, I was just trying to be polite. I should have left. But there are strict rules about leaving saunas or steam rooms. You can't leave as soon as you get in because you're then showing that you don't like the people already there while you can't leave when someone else comes in because that saying you don't like the person who's just arrived.

There is only a small window of opportunity to enter and leave a sauna without offending anyone else and that five minutes after sitting down and up to 30 seconds before you see anyone arriving.

Also, don't get me started with the awkwardness of sitting in a sauna when someone of the opposite sex comes in and you're the only person there. Do you stay, but then that might make them uncomfortable to be a sauna with a stranger? Or do you leave, but then that might make them think you're leaving because you don't like them?

It's a minefield.

That's why it's best just to sit. Even if the person you're sitting next to has their crown jewels on display. It's just polite to stay.

But still. If you are going to a sauna, please keep your clothes on.

FRIDAY 29 MARCH 2024 (REST)

I hadn't planned on resting today, instead, I was aiming for a bike session before dinner. But, when my wife had to go into work, and her two-hour estimate turned into five, I didn't have time to jump on the bike.

SATURDAY 30 MARCH 2024 (RUN)

On Thursday, I was invited to speak at a meeting of all our sales advisors. As today is Good Friday, and a holiday, and the last Friday in the month, which is a dress down day, I wore jeans and a jumper. However, I didn't realise that our advisors can't do that as they're meeting customers. I also didn't realise that while they don't have a uniform, they are asked to wear black for uniformity. I walked into a hotel meeting room, 20 people wearing black gathered around a table and buffet and all I could think was "I've just arrived at a wake". I only hoped that our sales director wasn't lying in a coffin at the front.

We're now at the strange time of year where dressing inappropriately is a given for any run. It may look like a nice spring day, but ninja showers can strike at any time while you're wearing just a t-shirt. While a cold wind, requiring tights and a jacket, can suddenly warm up if the sun comes out.

At least in winter, I know to wear everything. But now, the only consistency is always wearing the wrong thing. If I think it's cold, it will be warm, if I think it's warm, a blizzard will strike. Or like today, I go for a run, there's blue sky, and, five minutes later, there are hailstones. It was as appropriate as jeans at a funeral.

SUNDAY 31 MARCH 2024 (BIKE)

My bike faces a window, which faces our neighbour's garden, which faces southeast. As the clocks jumped forward an hour, I was up early and facing the rising sun for today's session. It was so bright, I thought of wearing shades. Indoor cycling, with shades?!!? Whatever next. Wearing waterproofs on a treadmill? I treated the sun the old-fashioned way – I squinted. It was only after I finished that I realised I could have just closed the blinds.

CHAPTER 6

DID NOT START: CELTMAN 2021

At the start of April 2021, the organisers announced Celtman would go ahead.

I was nervous. Swimming pools wouldn't reopen until the end of April and local lochs had only started to warm up and had yet to reach five degrees Celsius. Yet, just a few weeks later, I would need to swim two miles. It was a big ask and one that I worried about as I lacked training. I thought, at best, I would swim slowly, but that meant an increased risk of hypothermia and more chance I would tire myself out, later in the race.

To help prepare, Iain CeltBrother spotted that there was an opportunity for open water swimming in a canal lock. We were able to book a weekly session through to the end of May so we'd at least have one guaranteed swim a week. And I hoped it would be sunny for two months so that the water would heat up and I could get back to wild swimming too.

I hoped this last-minute effort would bring back some swimming ability before June. Because while the organisers had announced that Celtman would go ahead, I thought it was ambitious to hold it so soon after lockdown eased. Bold athletes may say that a lack of swim practice was just part of the 'extreme' nature of an 'extreme triathlon', but sometimes athletes need protected from themselves.

I remember sitting in the boat in San Francisco in 2017 waiting for the Escape from Alcatraz swim to start when the organisers announced it was cancelled due to high winds. The safety boats couldn't sail and there would be no one to protect the competitors. "It's okay," shouted one man, "I don't need a safety boat". However, some decisions need to be taken out of athlete's hands, especially when those hands haven't been in water since lockdown had returned in December 2020.

Despite my nerves, I did try. But, three weeks later, I couldn't lift my arms. Every time I tried and raised them a ripple of pain ran from my elbows to my shoulders. The same happened when I tried to lie on them in bed. Any weight left them throbbing and numb. After an hour of trying to get to sleep I got up and swallowed some painkillers before sitting in the living room waiting for Nurofen to kick in. It took three hours, 4am, before I could move an arm without hurting. I finally go back to bed cursing every stroke I swam that week as I tried to go from nothing to 2 kms in three weeks.

I persevered for a few more weeks. But by the end of May I was still struggling with a 2km swim, and I knew that it would be stupid to start Celtman. I did the smart thing and pulled out.

CHAPTER 7

APRIL

MONDAY 1 APRIL (REST)

What's the longest ultra-marathon in the world? I'd imagine it would involve crossing an entire country or jogging from one continent to another. Something EPIC. Something LOOOONNNG but also something achievable. A non-stop race would not need competitors to sleep. It could be no more than a few days before the race must end. I'm thinking of the Ultra Marathon Mont Blanc. 48 hours of running up and down the Swiss Alps.

However, if not continuous, if we're thinking a multi-stage ultra-marathon, then runners will still tire and runners will not be able to continue, even with some rest. I'm thinking of the Marathon De Sable and five days across the Sahara Desert.

However, the actual longest ultra-marathon is none of these things. It doesn't cross continents. It doesn't cross countries. It doesn't even cross the street. It's held entirely around one New York city block. It's the Sri Chinmoy Self-Transcendence 3100 Mile Race – and it takes place each June for around 50 days. Runners run around the same block every day from 6am to midnight clocking up around 60 miles each day.

I found this race after Iain CeltBrother ran his lap marathon last weekend: a marathon that involved 105 laps of a running track. I thought that was long, but I wondered if there were ultra-marathons that also involved running laps and that led me to find 12 and 24 hours races that involve competitors running as far as they can within the time-limit. And, as I fell down the internet rabbit hole of long-distance circling, I found the Sri Chinmoy Self-

Transcendence race.

I think there is a trend for further and more exotic events. Taking part in a fun run in your local park has been replaced by extreme triathlons in settings so remote you only see them on the Discovery challenge.

Instead, can we reverse the trend? Make races smaller and more local? Instead of the London marathon crossing the Thames and running from one end of the city to another, could runners instead run back and forth in front of Buckingham Palace until they reach 26.2 miles?

Equally, what's the point of most sprint stages at the Tour de France. It's four hours of flat cycling followed by 20 minutes of excitement at the end as the sprint team battle it out. Just ditch the whole scenic tour of France and go straight to the dash through an industrial suburb of Marseille.

As for Everest? Get a helicopter to drop you at the Edmund Hillary Step and just climb the last 20 metres. Easy.

TUESDAY 2 APRIL 2024 (BIKE)

"Why are you running 105 laps?" I asked Iain CeltBrother.

"It'll be fun," he said.

"No, it won't," I said, "it'll be boring. You need variety. You can't just do the same thing again and again and again."

"What about swimming?" He said.

"Good point."

So, today I did laps of the same climb on Zwift. Climb up, cycle down, turn around and climb again because laps are now cool.

WEDNESDAY 3 APRIL 2024 (REST)

Since Saturday, I've had a cold. It's not been serious, but as it developed into a cough and I decided to sweat it out in a sauna rather than try and run.

THURSDAY 4 APRIL 2024 (SWIM)

"Who wants to be the leader?" Asked Sean the Coach.

No one answered.

"Okay, Andrew, you can do it."

Damn.

It's normally the same people in my swimming lane each week and we know which of us is faster than the others and we can swim from fastest to slowest in the same order. Today, our fastest swimmer was on holiday, and we needed someone else to go first. I normally swim second or third so was 'promoted'.

I don't like swimming first as I don't like the pressure of having to count the correct laps. Counting laps is not cool. I do realise this is not the greatest pressure in the world. I'm not the US President deciding whether to launch a nuclear missile, or a footballer taking a penalty in a World Cup final, or someone who has ever been told by their wife "you decide" when you say you're popping to Tesco and you ask if they would like a sweet. You know, the real hard decisions.

However, I had to go first, which I did, counting badly, until about 20 minutes later the man behind me in second place passed me, and asked to take the lead.

"Absolutely," I said, a born follower.

But my relief didn't last long. He's overestimated his strength and was soon asking to move back as his arms were getting tired.

Damn.

I was leading again.

FRIDAY 5 APRIL 2024 (RUN)

Today was a 'BBC Weather App run'. Storm Kathleen was due to arrive today and last the weekend. The forecast predicted a hour of reasonable weather just before lunch, in between heavy rain and, later, heavy winds.

The forecast was right. I went for a run at 12 as the rain eased and was back just before it returned to biblical levels.

SATURDAY 6 APRIL 2024 (BIKE)

On. Off. On. Off. On. Off. On. Off. A bitty long ride that started at 8am with 1 hour and then continued after lunch with various sessions as I couldn't quite get into a settled routine.

Storm Kathleen was still overhead, and while it was warm and dry, I could see gusts of winds rattle the trees as I looked out from my static bike. I thought of going out and trying a route that would have the wind behind me, perhaps going to Edinburgh west to east and hitting a new land speed record. But I decided that riding in strong winds is not fun, even when trying to ride it like Wile E Coyote with a giant Acme fan on his back.

SUNDAY 7 APRIL 2024 (REST)

A swap day. I'm going to be in Inverness on Monday and wanted to run while I was there. I swapped today's run with tomorrow's rest so I can...

MONDAY 8 APRIL 2024 (RUN)

... run around Inverness. Running along the River Ness is one of my favourite running routes, in fact running anywhere near water is among my favourite things. Especially in Inverness as I also have a chance of seeing Nessie. I've not seen him (or her) yet. But you never know. One day he might just pop his head up and say "hello".

Today I ran first thing in the morning before work and ran back and forth along the bridges crossing the Ness. I like running on the various pedestrian bridges as it feels like running on a trampoline. The bridges need to be flexible to cope with wind so there's always a little sway and give as you run, which makes running feel like Godzilla stomping through New York or Nessie going for a jog along the loch.

TUESDAY 9 APRIL 2024 (BIKE)

The problem with jumping on the bike straight after work is that other people don't know you've finished work. Tonight, I had five calls after 5pm and I'm too much of a workaholic to ignore them. I also have standards, so I stop cycling to take the call. It seems rude to carry on and have a conversation with all the sounds of a heavy breathing pervert.

Because of the interruptions, it felt like a very broken session. And while I was aiming to cycle for longer, by the time I finished it felt like I'd only been cycling 20 minutes, which was right, as it had only been 20 mins from my fifth and final call.

WEDNESDAY 10 APRIL 2024 (REST)

A tricky day to fit in training as I had to travel to another office and look after CeltChild while my wife went to London. Her meeting was cancelled, and she was able to come home but by that point I'd already ordered fish and chips. Training was out, eating was in.

THURSDAY 11 APRIL 2024 (SWIM)

The good thing about my wife's meeting being cancelled was that she was home overnight, and I could go swimming in the morning. Another longest swim to date and I'm starting to feel confident in my swimming for the race. Next step though is to start swimming outdoors.

The last time I swam outdoors was in Gourock outdoor pool in August last year. Gourock Outdoor Pool is Scotland's oldest heated swimming pool – and the only one to feature on number one album cover. It was used as the cover image for Blur's 'The Life of Darren'.

Gourock is on the west coast of Scotland is not to be confused with its next-door neighbour, Greenock. You can tell the difference between the two because only one regularly features in crime reports (Greenock), the other (Gourock) is used as an album cover. They may be side by side on the Clyde coast, but Gourock is the 'better' of the two. And as for their third neighbour, Port Glasgow... well, it's where the criminals of Greenock fear to go at night…

Gourock Outdoor Pool is a good place to practice outdoor

swimming as the pool uses sea water and the first thing you'll notice when you swim is the taste of salt. More important, the pool is heated, yes, heated, to feel like a nice dip on a warm summer's day, which is not something that can be said about Celtman and the west coast of Scotland.

I made one mistake when I swam last year. I started swimming and was sure I'd swum 1,000 metres only to check my watch to find it was just 700m. I tried again and again I was short. It was only as I was leaving that a man mentioned that the pool was 33m and not 25m. I'd set my watch to record 25m laps.

FRIDAY 12 APRIL 2024 (RUN)

Timing is everything. At Celtman you have 13 hours to get to the start of Beinn Eighe. You need to complete the swim, complete the bike, and run 12 miles within 13 hours otherwise you don't get to start the final section. During that time, you also need to eat. Most people don't eat during the swim section as it's tricky to eat a banana in the middle of the sea, while batting away jelly fish. Most people eat during the bike and run legs. They may have gels or snacks, but rarely will they have a full meal. Though I once had a cheese sandwich halfway through the IronMan bike leg; I have not seen anyone else take a Pret A Manger approach to nutrition. But, if you get the chance to try it, after umpteen gels and energy drinks there is nothing as tasty as a bit of cheese. You don't even need to have the bread, just stick a chunk of cheddar in your pocket and munch on it when you get to the 50 mile point, you will be blown away.

Timing is everything with eating and training runs too. I like to run to work in the morning however I need to time breakfast carefully. You can't run on a full stomach of Weetabix. You need to let things settle. And how long to leave it depends on how long you're going to run. If only a few miles, then 30 mins is okay. If 5 miles or more, then best to leave it at least an hour.

This morning was an early run so I had my breakfast and then pottered about for 30 minutes before I started my run.

SATURDAY 13 APRIL 2024 (RUN)

I don't run two days in a row that often. I don't mind swimming or cycling on consecutive days but, with running, if I run for two days, I can feel my legs getting stiffer and heavier on the third day. When training, I know if I run on alternate days then it doesn't impact any other training.

However, today was a chance to go for a longer run with Iain CeltBrother and to have an easier run as he trains for his next race, an Ultramarathon in May, and runs a minute slower than my current pace.

"You could run at my pace," I said.

"Are you running 50km in three weeks," he said.

"No."

"Then we run at my pace!" He said.

I didn't argue.

SUNDAY 14 APRIL 2024 (BIKE)

It is a truth universally acknowledged that if you fall off your bike the first thing you will say is "It's okay, I'm alright!".

When the Tour De France crashes in a cross wind and forty riders lie in a crumpled heap in the middle of a daffodil field, they will all leap back up and try and get back on their bike, even the ones with a broken leg, a missing arm and no head. What is it about bike injuries that makes us ignore the fountain of blood arcing from our bloodied stumps?

I've fallen off my bike several times. I even had one passer-by force me to go to hospital after they saw me fall, yet the only thing I said to the casualty nurse was "I feel fine now!".

I think it's the shame factor. Falling off a bike is embarrassing so, when it happens, we try and cover up the shame by pretending everything is okay and there's nothing to see. Please move on. Don't call 999. I can stick my foot back on with a couple of plasters.

I say this as last night, when walking the dog, a cyclist tried to cycle around us on a path, slid on a bit of mud, and then fell face first on the pavement in front of us.

"Are you okay?" We asked.

Which is a stupid question. Of course they're not okay. They've just face planted concrete paving. That's going to hurt even as they say: "It's okay, I'm alright."

They said this as blood dripped down their face from their bloodied nose.

"Are you sure?"

Again, a stupid question. No one dripping blood is okay. Especially if it's your own, and even more so if it's someone else's.

"Yes, I'm fine," they said as they got back on the bike.

"Would you like a tissue?" I asked, as I had a tissue in my pocket, albeit it was one that had been there for some time and had seen two colds worth of bogeys.

"No," they said, quite wisely. Who accepts a hankie from a stranger? It would be cleaner to lick the back seat of a bus.

"Okay," I said, not sure of what else to do. In the Tour De France someone would give the injured rider a push as they start again but I thought this was not the time or the place or the moment to put my hand on their bum and give it a shove.

"I'm fine," they insisted before riding off, leaving a bloody blood breadcrumb trail behind them.

As they rode away, I looked at the spot they fell. We were on a path with a wall on one side and a fence on the other. The side of the path were covered in mud and, looking at it again, I could have left more room for them to pass.

"Do you think we caused them to fall?" asked Mrs Celtwife.

"It's okay, it's wasn't us." I lied. But, of course, we'd caused the accident. If we hadn't been standing there the cyclist would never have cycled on the mud. However, I don't think we're responsible for it. Riding on mud is stupid and stupidity is the number one cause of most accidents.

At the end of last year, I lost my drone. I was flying it near a dam, trying to fly it along the main pipe and up to the falling water off the dam sluice when I received a warning that I was running low on battery. I checked the battery, and it said I had three mins flight time left. I thought that was plenty of time to continue for another shot and then fly it back to me. I was wrong. 90 seconds later the drone screen flashed red, the drone began it's automatic descent to land and I tried desperately to work out where in the moor it might be so I could run over and collect it. 30 minutes later and after much trampling of heather, I found it. I should never have ignored the warning. I was an idiot. I was lucky to find it. But I was still an idiot.

Most injuries are the same. We might not have a red warning light but most times, when we look back, we might as well have, as the warning lights will have been flashing.

At Christmas, I fell off my bike. This is the third time I've fallen off in five years. Even worse, two of the times happened at the same place. To fall off one's bike in one place is an accident, to fall off one's bike in exactly the same place and in exactly the same conditions is no longer an accident, it's a trip to a consultant to get my head examined as I must have knocked all the sense out of it when I landed on it the first time.

I was in Carron Valley, it was cold, there was frost and ice on the road, and, despite falling here four years ago, I still tried to cycle when figure skating was the better option. I managed to get around 100m before I wobbled. That was my warning light. I continued. Two seconds later, I fell and banged my head on the road. What an idiot!

With other injuries, I can see the warning signs clearly, with hindsight. A cracked rib from trying to leap across a river when I should have turned round and returned home. I only continued because I hate running out and back. Instead, I ran out and walked back... clutching my rib.

Snapping an ankle ligament? The warning sign was there. I was 35 and playing fives football. Playing football after 35 is a warning sign. You don't need any more warning of impending injury than a desire to wear a replica football top while shouting "Pass! Pass! I'm free! I'm free!".

The signs are always there. If you want to avoid injury, just be less stupid.

MONDAY 15 APRIL 2024 (REST)

Feet up. A trip to the steam room. A man is sitting naked in the room. Well, technically, not naked. He has a towel around his waist, but the towel is so wet that it has become translucent. He tried to adjust the towel to better cover himself but all the happens is a butcher is wrapping sausage and meatballs in cellophane. I go to the sauna instead.

TUESDAY 16 APRIL 2024 (BIKE)

I love Frosties. They're great. But I can't have them because, once I have one bowl, I have to finish the entire packet. My name is Andrew Todd and I am a frostaholic.

Instead, for the last few years, I've had a bowl of All Bran. A cereal that looks like a thatched roof, tastes like a thatched roof and could be used to thatch a roof if a thatcher ever runs short of straw.

All Bran is meant to make you regular so, if Frosties can be said to be great, and Coco Pops can be said to make the mile go chocolately, the All Bran be said to make you shite yourself faster. Which is marketing slogans go, is not the best, I'll give you that. But, once you take away it's bowel benefits, what else can you say about All Bran? If Jacob Rees Mogg was a cereal, he would be All Bran, I think that's it.

That's why it's become harder and harder to motivate myself with breakfast when I cycle first thing. Normally, while riding, I will think, "I can't wait for breakfast!" But, with All Bran, it the breakfast equivalent of a queueing at the Post Office. It doesn't inspire me to pedal faster to get to my plate. I need a new cereal for Celtman, one

I can look forward to each morning, one that will inspire me rather than one that feels like a prescription. I need Frosties.

WEDNESDAY 17 APRIL 2024 (REST)

Packed my running kit. Trainers in the boot. All set to run straight after driving home from working in Larbert. Except I had to work late and lost all the time I was going to use to run as I only had a short window before I needed to be at home to look after Celtchild, as Mrs Celtwife Diary was in London and we would be on our own tonight.

THURSDAY 18 APRIL 2024 (RUN)

When do you change your running shoes? According to the shoe manufacturer, Asics, you should change them every 400 – 500 miles or earlier if sections of the rubber outsole are so worn that you can see the softer foam underneath or the midsole feels too soft and collapses easily under pressure or, my favourite, one or both shoes no longer stand up straight when placed on a flat surface.

However, I've got a simpler system to know when to replace your shoes: once a year, when the sales are on – or earlier, if a hole appears.

The important thing though is to change them whether they need changed or not – because no shoe lasts two years. If you get one year out of them, then you're doing well. If you get longer, even better. Because you can buy the new pair and then keep wearing the old pair until the hole appears.

It's a simple system and it's never failed me. Modern shoes should last a year, unless you are Kipchoge and running marathons every second week. But, in his case, he gets shoes for free from Nike so doesn't have to think about it. Mo Farah on the other hand, now that his career is slowing down faster than he is, will need to start thinking about buying his own. So, Mo, if you're reading, perhaps best you pop down to the January sales and buy a pair for this year.

So, there you go, you don't need to know much about shoes to keep injury free with proper trainers. Just buy one pair a year in the January sales and you'll never need to think about it again.

Unless you're training for Celtman and the hole starts to appear in April rather than December and my shoes wobble wobble when placed on a flat surface.

Are there any Spring sales?

FRIDAY 19 APRIL 2024 (BIKE/SWIM)

An easy bike ride first thing before the house wakes up then a swim later to catch up on missing yesterday's swim.

If I swim on a Friday, one of the lanes is used by a coach who teaches young children to swim. A couple of years ago I asked him about lessons. He asked how old my child was and I realised then that he didn't take adults, which was a pity as he looks to be a patient and decent coach. Today, I met him in the changing room, and he warned me that traffic wardens were targeting the streets around the pool. It was good of him to warn me, but he didn't know I had my system: I don't pay for parking, I only pay fines.

So, when I was told to watch out for traffic wardens, I thanked the swim coach as it was nice thing to do to warn a stranger, but all I thought was "I've parked enough times to pay for ten tickets now and still make a profit!"

SATURDAY 22 APRIL 2024 (RUN)

110 days. Almost a third of the year and finally, finally, finally, not only is not raining, and not only is there a bright blue sky, it's also warm. Genuinely warm. Like wearing a puffer jacket but not actually having the jacket on. It's pleasant. And nice. And I don't know how to react as I run round. I'm used to wearing a running jacket – I had one on Thursday - and now I'm running in just a t-shirt.

The rest of Glasgow doesn't know how to react either. Picnic blankets have bloomed in the park like Spring daffodils. It's not picnic weather, it's warm but it's not Summer warm – puffer jacket and a fleece warm – but the park is filled with people sitting and enjoying the first and, 110 days into this year, only sign of Spring.

SUNDAY 23 APRIL 2024 (BIKE)

Which didn't last to the weekend. I thought Sunday was to be a repeat of Saturday so hasn't checked the weather forecast. I was also out – yes, outside on a bike – first thing because I had to be back for 10am and I wanted to get a long ride in before that.

So, with thoughts of a new early morning sunshine I jumped on my bike, started riding north out of Glasgow and towards Strathblane, and wished I'd pulled on a pair of gloves as the cold wind cut into my hands. Then it started to drizzle and stayed that way for the rest of the ride.

The one thing that riding indoors can't teach you: weather.

Maybe I can get Mrs Celtwife to pour a bucket of water on my head to get ready for the Scottish summer?

MONDAY 24 APRIL 2024 (REST)

David Beckham is famous for many things. Whether it scoring from the half way line; getting sent off against Argentina; wearing pants for cash; starring in ads about Qatar for cash; or just being David Beckham (and not Sir David) for cash, he's done so many things it's hard to pick out just the one thing to remember him for.

However, if I had to choose, the one thing I remember about David Beckham is that no one ever broke a foot until David Beckham broke his foot. Which is strange. He plays FOOTball. He's a FOOTballer. He kicks the ball with his FOOT. But, until he broke his foot in the run up to the 2002 World Cup, no one had ever heard of the word "metatarsal", yet, afterwards it become a common football injury and every club has a player with a broken metatarsal, which, if you don't know, is the bones that go from the base of the toes back towards the arch of the foot. The metatarsal bones form the weight-bearing part of the foot.

So, thanks, David Beckham, you not only married a Spice Girl, you also invented a whole new field of sporting injury. It should really be called the Beckham bones, in honour of the great man himself.

I say all this because last year I had an emergency visit to Hampden Sports Clinic who confirmed that I was just like David Beckham. "One of the most handsome men on the planet?" I asked. "No," they said, "you have a metatarsal injury."

I'd been on holiday and had missed a long run on Easter Sunday and had ran instead on Easter Monday. I was training and have been gradually increasing my miles run each week until, that day, I ran 12 miles only to find myself unable to walk a few hours later.

Every time I tried to place weight on my left foot I could feel a dull pain stretching from my middle toe around the left hand side of my foot and down to my heel.

I did what all athletes do in these circumstances. I walked three miles to try and walk it off.

It didn't work.

I tried my back up plan. I left it overnight and then tried walking three miles again. That didn't work either. Onto plan C. Speak to a specialist.

I booked into the Hampden Sports Clinic to speak to a podiatrist. And he confirmed that I was on the right track – as he made me walk back and forth along a corridor, which was shorter than three miles, but he did say "this is to see if it still hurts".

He then made me run on a treadmill. "Does this hurt?" He asked. "No," I said. So he turned up the speed until it did.

Then he poked at various points on my foot again asking, "Does this hurt?" and I couldn't help thinking it would be much nicer if he said "Is this okay?" to confirm a positive rather than a negative. But medical professional prefer to know when they're causing pain rather than when they are helping. Dicks.

After an hour he proclaimed that I had a stress injury, that it was unlikely to be muscular or a fracture and that I should stop running or two weeks and then try again to see if it hurts.

Two weeks was a frustrating prescription but better to take two weeks off than developing a worse injury later. And, thanks to David Beckham, I had a far cooler sounding metatarsal injury rather than the old fashioned and very uncool name of "tippy toe injury"

I mention this now because it's almost a year since I injured myself and it turned out to be closer to eight weeks rather than two before I could run again. So, with so far injury free training, I enter this week with my most ambitious week yet: my first bike race on Saturday and a 10k to finish this week. Two races in two days, which is easier than three races in one day, but it should give me a good idea of how much more I need to do in the next two months before Celtman. Fingers crossed; I don't get injured.

TUESDAY 23 APRIL 2024 (RUN)

Near the Barrowlands, a music venue on the edge of the city centre, there is a path listing every band to ever play there, along with the date of their concert. I like to run along it and catch a glimpse of concerts I've seen but had forgotten all about. I remember Radiohead, I remember the Manic Street Preachers, I forgot about The Vines but then I catch a glimpse of their name on a step and I remember going to see them only to see a band where the lead singer was strung out on drugs and the show was only 30 minutes long, thankfully. It was awful.

But as I ran further east, I ran past the Barras market and then the People's Palace before running onto the edge of Glasgow Green only to see more words on the ground in front of me. Every third pavement stone had "Edge of Green" inscribed on it. And I could think was: "I don't remember them playing the Barrowlands."

I assume the words are there to show the boundary of Glasgow Green, the largest park in Glasgow. And the words are needed as a road now runs along what I thought was the edge of the park but must run along the inside of the park and the pavement is there to show the true boundary.

You can see a similar boundary line in London and New York, particularly around tall buildings. Small bumps on the ground will show the boundary of the tower. Often, if you look up, you'll find the edge of the building overhead. Not a metre of space is waste.

I'd never seen such markings in Glasgow and it was fun to run along the true edge of the park and to find a historic part of the city I never knew existed.

WEDNESDAY 24 APRIL 2024 (RUN)

Running at an average pace and in the shortest direction from home to work takes around 28 minutes. If I get the train then I would leave the house five minutes before the train leaves the station, and it would take me another five minutes at the end to walk to work. The journey itself is 15 minutes. The challenge I asked myself this morning, as Mrs Celtwife left to catch the train, and I left to run to work is whether I could catch up with her in town as she walked to her work (which is near my office) or whether she would get in first. Man v Train v Wife.

Wife won.

THURSDAY 25 APRIL 2024 (SWIM)

"Swim buoys are sexist," she explained to Sean the coach, "woman have wider hips. If I use a buoy then it raises my body and it's too high in the water. It would be easier to swim without the buoy, than with it."

I love swimming with a buoy because it makes it easier for me to swim. If I'm not kicking my legs, it feels easier. I never realised it would be different for girls. I just assumed that it was the same for everyone. Boys, like me, it turns out, can be sexist too.

FRIDAY 26 APRIL 2024 (GOLF)

Last year someone recommended that I read 'Dream On' by John Richardson, the story of how one hopeless golfer tried to become a brilliant golfer in just 12 months.

He set himself a challenge – he would play a perfect round of golf. He'd shoot a level par round – a round of 18 holes, where he equalled or bettered the course score without the help of any extra strokes. The only problem he had was that he started the year as a hopeless golfer who needed 20 extra strokes or more to get round.

Did he do it? Normally in these types of books the pleasure of reading it is to find out whether the author was successful... or not...

But, spoiler alert...

The author gives the game away in the first few chapters by randomly including a sentence starting with "After I did it..."

Thanks, John - or your sub-editor for that spoiler. Apart from that, what did I learn from it and how could it apply to triathlon? I learned that it training was not about 'the glamour'.

John made the mistake for most of his training of concentrating on his first shot – the drive. He wanted to hit the ball further and faster and with a bigger THWACK than anyone else. The drive is what impresses your playing partners and your club mates. It's the most visible part of being a good golfer. The big shot from the tee.

However, for over six months he didn't practice putting. The sedate cousin of driving. There's no big swing. No THWACK. It's a gentle motion that seemingly requires no skill even though holing a long putt is one of the main things every golf programme focuses on in their daily highlights. It's the glamour shot no one notices.

Yet, for John, it was only when he started to concentrate on his putting that his score started to improve because it wasn't just one skill, it's multiple skills. You need to be able to drive, you need to be able to hit a long iron for your second shot, you need to pitch short shots around the green and then you need to put. Also, you need to keep all your womanising quiet, but that's just Tiger Woods.

It's the same for triathlon. The skills bit. Not the womanising bit. Triathlon is a mix of skills. From swimming to cycling to running and all important getting your wet suit off quickly in transition without falling over.

Yet, to improve, do we spend the same amount of time on all four parts?

If you're anything like me then you concentrate on the bits that are easy – the running and cycling – and work less on the bits that are hard. To improve we need to concentrate on all parts.

Which seems obvious but it's worth repeating because it's easy to get seduced by the quick fixes that triathlon offers. A new wet suit, a faster bike, when all that matters is concentrating on the basics. Swim technique, pedalling and moving your feet faster for long than you did before.

Oh, and not falling over when trying to pull your wetsuit of your legs.

Anyway, all this came to mind because, today I went golfing when my training diary said running. I rarely play golf, and I never practice, and I haven't improved in 15 years. Just think how better I would get if I actually tried?

SATURDAY 27 APRIL 2024 (BIKE)

And the week started so ambitiously with my goal of taking part in the Kinross Sportive. However, I didn't take account of the weather and with a forecast for rain later in the day I changed plans and cycled to Edinburgh via Falkirk, Linlithgow, Bo'Ness and South Queensferry instead, leaving first thing in the morning to dodge the rain. More fool me though, I may have avoided the rain, but I caught the overnight freeze and left as the thermometer struggled to get above zero. I spent the first hour using every traffic light to rub my hands and blow warm air onto them to try and get some life back in my fingers.

As my longest ride outdoors (not a strong competition given I only started going outdoors last weekend), it was a good test for my bike fitness. I was pleased to cycle for over five hours on just a handful of gels and some water without feeling too tired. By the end, the hardest part was sitting down. My ass started to chafe from my saddle, but my legs still felt strong and the ride gave me a good confidence boost with seven weeks to go to Celtman.

My important lesson though was one that I should have figured out much earlier: the main difference between cycling indoors and outdoors is simple – downhill sections. When riding indoors, I have to peddle all the time to keep moving. When cycling outdoors, I can coast while I going downhill.

Now, if only Celtman was downhill?

SUNDAY 28 APRIL 2024 (RUN)

If only today's run was downhill. Heavy legs today. I woke up intending to run before breakfast but I changed my mind and decided a late afternoon run would be better after a bit of a rest and a good breakfast and lunch for some energy. Even so, I was running a minute per mile slower than my last run and every step felt sluggish and weighty. A good week of training but I'm looking forward to a rest day tomorrow.

MONDAY 29 APRIL 2024 (REST)

My first sporting memory is watching a team in green and white winning the Scottish Cup against a team in orange. I loved football and wanted to follow the team that won. They were Celtic and that was about the only thing they won in the next fifteen years as their rivals, Rangers, dominated Scottish football until 2000. I didn't know it at the time but choosing Celtic in the Western Isles was like ordering a steak in a vegan restaurant. Everyone on the island supported Rangers because the Isle of Lewis is to protestants what the Vatican is to Catholics.

Lewis is a very religious island. Sunday or the Sabbath is a holy day and no shops would open, the swings in playparks would be tied up and even clothes lines would be cut if anyone dared to hang their underwear out on the Lord's day.

It was tediously DULL.

Imagine a day when nothing happened. Slowly. And not just a day because the Stornoway Sabbath started when the minister went to bed on a Saturday night, and it didn't end until he got up on a Monday morning.

And nothing could happen because, unless you were going to church, everything else was banned. Even watching TV was banned, though not in our house as while Sunday School was compulsory, our Dad still wanted to watch Scotsport on a Sunday teatime.

It was only in recent years that the airport and ferry opened to allow people to leave the island on a Sunday. We inadvertently ended up on the first Sunday sailing. We were in Stornoway, saw there was a Sunday sailing and booked it not knowing it was the first. At the ferry terminal there were 20 people in black suits and heavy tweed coats silently protesting – because, naturally, on Sunday, shouting was banned. Beside them there were a hundred people clapping to show their support for the new service. On board we hid below deck, while we supported the new service, we didn't want to be in the photo they'd use in the local paper under the headline "Heathens Leave Island. Destination: Hell!".

When I came back to Stornoway from university, I always loved the Stornoway sabbath. It provides a day each week when you know you don't need to do anything. However, the Stornoway version was too extreme. If it was sunny outside you couldn't play football, you still can't play golf. Today, I'll go for a run but twenty years ago even that would have been frowned on. Even if you didn't go to church yourself, you still cared what your neighbours thought and respected their beliefs.

In many ways growing up in Stornoway was a glimpse not just into the past but into an older past too. While the mainland moved with the times and Sunday became the weekend rather than a special day itself, Stornoway remembered when the Sabbath meant something. It was a reminder that you should spend one day a week doing something different, whether it be resting, praying or tying up children's swings (lest Satan tempt them to swing on the Sabbath).

There's a lesson here for triathletes. The need for a rest day or days. A reminder that it's just as important to stop as it is to start. And pushing to do something every day is not always progress. A useful lesson as I enter the final weeks of Celtman training and try to get the last benefits of my training.

TUESDAY 30 APRIL 2024 (BIKE)

There are 14 billion videos on YouTube and I have watched all of them. And, with a three-year-old, I have watched all the Peppa Pig videos more than once.

I jumped on the bike before work for an easy session and switched on YouTube to watch something as I rode. However, there was nothing to watch, my Watch Later playlist was empty, I've watched everything I wanted to watch. There was nothing left. I would have to come up with something else to watch beyond videos of landscape photographers who make videos of the places they go and the photos they take, videos about how films are made, and Late Night with Seth Myers. Would I now have to watch Jimmy Fallon? Or, God forbid, Mr Beast?

This is something that no training manual will ever tell you. You can spend so long training indoors that you will eventually run out of things to watch.

CHAPTER 8

SUPPRT: CELTMAN 2022

For someone who loves wearing a wetsuit, I hate getting wet.

The first time I was soaked while running was at the Helensburgh half marathon during a day where it was impossible to tell where the sea ended and Helensburgh began. The puddles were so deep that trident submarines were using them for dive practice. It was a grim, grim day.

Yet, I ran anyway and my only thought the entire way round was to run as fast as I could so that I could get back to the car, back home and to never venture outside again. With such a thought, I ended up running my fastest ever half marathon – and my fastest ever medal collection as I didn't stop at the finish line, I just kept going straight through, grabbed a medal, and sprinted back to the car.

The second time I was properly soaked was during the Three Peaks Challenge. We started at Ben Nevis and it was so wet that you could practically swim to the summit. It was impossible to stay dry even in thick waterproofs. By the time I got to the summit I pulled off my sodden gloves only to discover flippers instead of fingers. It was a grim, grim day.

The third and last time I was properly soaked was during the Celtman 2022 run route. I was acting as support runner for Iain CeltBrother and, thankfully, I had assumed that by the time I joined him, he'd be knackered and would be walking rather than running. As such, I brought my full mountain gear rather than trail running clothes. A thick waterproof jacket instead of a packable one. Gloves so thick you could pick up radioactive blocks at Chernobyl. And a pair of full length trousers rather than waterproof shorts.

This time the rain was on and off but, as we walked, the rain spells would last longer and stronger until, eventually, I was soaked through again. Another, grim, grim day.

So, the lesson I want to pass one is not the one about rain making you run faster (which it does) or always be prepared for the weather for more equipment or clothes than you think you need (and more again, you can never have enough clothes where you're cold and wet), it's a simple one: move to somewhere it doesn't rain.

What's the connection between my three tales? They all happened in Scotland. Scotland is a grim, grim place! Why not live in Dubai? The Sahara or even the middle of Death Valley? It never rains there.

But what else do you need to know about acting as support for Celtman?
In 2022, Iain was successful in the ballot and I was unsuccessful at dodging his request to be his skivvy/butler/lackey/dogsbody for the day by acting as both his support driver and runner.

Conditions for Iain Celtbrother at Celtman were brutal. 3K swim, 120 mile bike and a marathon in 40mph headwinds and driving rain. However, I can report, at least at the start line with a duvet and pillow, the support car was roasty toasty.

Competitors need to register in Sheildaig and board the bus to the start line by 4am. There's no access to the swim start for supporters so, once you've helped them set up at transition and register there's nothing to do but keep warm and wait until they return to shore from 6am onwards. One of the local cafes was open, so there is an opportunity for some food or a hot drink, but

I just used the time to try and catch up on sleep. We were up at 2:30am with a target of leaving the AirBnB at 2:45am so I'd only had a few hours sleep.

Sleep wasn't helped by Iain Celtbrother booking a pre-race base with no curtains. It was a night of trying to sleep while it was still as bright as noon outside. That's part of why I brought a duvet and pillow to the start. As I waited for Iain's to finish the swim I was perfectly set (and warm) in the car for another 90 minutes kip.

The swim exit itself was easy to find – it's the one surrounded by supporters, braziers of fire and a drum troupe. You can't miss it in Sheildaig. And with the drums banding away, you probably couldn't miss in half the western Highlands.

You need your support t-shirt to access the exit and transition. Remember to wear it as, with it, you can get onto the shore and help your competitor over the rocky beach and up to transition.

After you help them change, you pack up everything, pick up your car and you have a couple of hours before you can join them again. You're not allowed to support competitors during the first 15 miles of the race. I used this time to go back to base, eat some breakfast, pick up Mrs Celtwife and Celtchild and ensure the car had everything for the rest of the day.

We met Iain Celtbrother around three hours after he started. We then tried to meet him roughly every 45 – 60 mins. He didn't always stop but we wanted to give him the chance to pick up food or drink or to change into or out of his waterproof clothes.

The thing to watch out for on the bike course is that many parking spots are slightly off the road requiring you to pull in, rather than parking at the side of the road itself. It's particularly tricky to find a spot on the road between Ullapool and Garve. So, you may want to agree in advance the spots you'll meet.

Other than that, the support cars are well spread out and

there was plenty of room for everyone on the road. I had been concerned that the Gairloch coastal road may have seen some bottlenecking but there were no issues at all.

Car parking at Kinlochewe however was challenging: parking was in a field. A muddy field. A very muddy field. A local farmer had to pull some cars out of the field with a tractor as they struggled to get through mud at the entrance. Luckily, we were directed to park just outside the field so had no problems but a lot of people were struggling and panicking about how they were going to get to the transition without a car to take them there.

At the transition for the second half of the run, there's no shelter, just a Portaloo. This year, that meant I had to change into all my warm clothes and waterproofs while waiting for Iain Celtbrother to arrive. This was okay as it was largely dry while I waited with only a few brief showers. However, if it's a decent day then you'll normally be arriving here around peak midge times. So, if there weather is decent, prepare face the might of a million Scottish midges as you wait. Luckily, we avoided the midges because even midges don't go out when God turns his rain sprinkler setting to: "fill a swimming pool quickly" mode.

Even in Summer, Scotland can be in the middle of winter. A useful lesson in how bad it can get on the west coast and a warning for this year to be prepared for anything.

CHAPTER 9

MAY

WEDNESDAY 1 MAY 2024 (RUN)

Legs recovered from Sunday, a decent pace and the sun was out. This is what training should be like. It's just a pity that in Scotland it takes five months to get to this point. My only niggle is a sharp pain in my foot but I've noticed it only happens when wearing my trail running trainers (which are waterproof) and not my normal road running trainers. It feels like a razer across the ball of my foot. I think it must be the trainers and not the injury as it doesn't happen at any other time.

Even so, I do the standard running thing of ignoring it. Running with an injury should just be called 'running'. Runners are always injured.

Ask any runner and they can talk for hours about their creaky knees, dodgy ankles and wonky hips. "But it's always been like that!" They'll add, forgetting that it wasn't like that before they started running.

Runners are basically the Black Knight from Monty Python and the Holy Grail. Despite how many limbs are chopped off the knight still cries 'tis but a flesh wound!' and battles on.

That's why there are certain stages that runners go through when they run with injuries... sorry... when they run normally. At the moment I have a pain in my left foot. It falls into the category that I call "It Doesn't Get Any Worse When I Run".

This is an injury that's just as sore when you walk as when you run. That mean, and this is logical, I can run because running doesn't make it any worse! (Don't think about the logic, just trust me!)

These types of injury also tend to fall into the related category of... 'It Doesn't Get Any Worse If I Run On Alternative Days'. Again the logic here is sound. If the injury doesn't get any worse because you only ran on a Monday and Wednesday then clearly you can't be injured at all. An injury would hurt all the time so, if it only hurts on alternate days then it can't be an injury at all. Simple.

But if it escalates it can become an 'After Five Minutes It Doesn't Hurt When I Run'. This is a tricky injury because it does hurt when you run. Usually quite painfully and in a way which suggest amputation may be in your future. However, after five minutes, all the pain goes away! (Though it does tend to return an hour after you stop – and ten times worse than it was before).

I've had this injury. I hurt my knee and every time I tried to run it would be very painful to put any weight on my leg for the first five minutes then everything was okay until I stopped and had to cry with the pain of it all.

However, as it wasn't sore when I ran, or at least most of the time, it wasn't an injury at all...

If you have an 'It Hurts When I Lie Down' injury then - wimp! If it only hurts when you lie down, then you know what to do – go for a run.

And if 'It Hurts All The Time' then, at this point, a runner may admit this could be an injury and will book an appointment to see a physio in three week's time. In the meantime: keep running. You never know, it might heal on it's own.

THURSDAY 2 MAY 2024 (SWIM)

ANDREW TODD

People say that golf's a "good walk spoiled" but, as I like golf, I prefer to say that swimming's a "good drowning spoiled".

Swimming is a silly sport.

Think about it. You don't have running events where we move our legs in different ways. We don't have the 100m normal run, the 100m bandy leg run – nor do we run 100m backwards. Yet, swimming thinks it's perfectly okay to have umpteen different ways of thrashing your arms to make you go forward – or backwards.

Shouldn't the person who swims 100 meters fastest be the person who... you know... swims 100 meters the fastest? Stop giving gold medals to people who are not fast enough to swim fast enough.

Swimmers know they shouldn't reward second place. There's a hierarchy in swimming. At the top they have 'free style' and at the bottom they have 'doggy paddle' a stroke so poor they don't even call it a stroke, they call it a paddle, a name which comes from having to use a boat because you can't swim. And this hierarchy is clear because although swimmers have free style events where swimmers can swim any of the four main stokes – freestyle, backstroke, breaststroke and butterfly – they all swim freestyle because it's the fastest.

You wouldn't race Uisean Bolt by jogging, not sprinting, so you don't race free style by using any stroke other than the fastest.

Yet, still we celebrate Michael Phelps even though he's not actually got as many gold medals as you think because many of those medals are for events where, even though he came first, he was still not the fastest man to swim from one side of a pool to another.

Perhaps my views on swimming are based on the fact that I'm just jealous. Swimming is hard. I enjoy it, but it's hard.

For years I could only swim breaststroke. But, when I entered my first triathlon, I knew I would have to learn to swim free style – and I struggled.

The first lap would be okay, the second not bad, the third was when my lungs gave out, the water leaked into my goggles and into my eyes and, by the time I'd reached the fourth lap I was knackered.

It took a few months to become even vaguely confident about swimming and, even now, a few years later, while I've grown to like swimming, I don't love it the same way I love running and cycling. I love it more.

While I started because it's part of triathlon and a major part of Celtman, since I've been going to these coached sessions I feel comfortable swimming for an hour and taking on faster sessions or longer swims. I look forward to going to the pool and it doesn't feel like a chore. I've even signed up for the next swim sessions covering the weeks after Celtman as I plan to keep going after the race.

Swimming, maybe, is not a silly sport after all.

FRIDAY 3 MAY 2024 (RUN)

Big day for Celtdog as he was due at the vets to get a scalpel applied to his bum, but not for a Brazilian bumlift, he had a growth which needed to be cut off. A bum flap operation. Though I suspect that's not how the vet described it. I know, because, when I brought Celtdog to the vet a few weeks ago, they didn't use the words "bum" or "flap". They called an "arse-ectomy", because they are doctors. (Animal doctors).

With CeltDog going in for his buttock butchery, a trip to Edinburgh at night, and a need to pick him up post operation, I only had lunchtime to run and only 30 minutes spare to do so. No choice then, I had to run like my dog's ass depended on it.

SATURDAY 4 MAY 2024 (BIKE)

Checking my cupboard and I found my tri-suit. Or fat suit, as it really should be call. Tri-suits are not flattering. Every imperfection is highlighted when it's covered by lycra. That's why, when I go to a race, I always admire anyone who would wear one because it requires a level of body confidence I don't possess. I'd much rather have a tri-burlap sack.

But, at races, among the 'normal' athletes you will also find the men and women who couldn't crease a suit even if they breathed out after eating a dozen Krispy Kreme donuts. The Kreme de la Kreme of triathletes. The ones you can't help but admire if you end up running, cycling or swimming behind them.

I don't notice these physical gods at any other time. I don't think "oh my, what broad shoulders he has" or "what a slim waist she has" at any other time. They only catch my eye at races and only with a tri-suit. That's why I think I might be… ahem… tri-sexual.

What I won't be is wearing my tri-suit. A quick check in the mirror and I can see a profile that has more lumps and bumps than the Celtman bike route. In any case, wearing a tri suit is all about wearing a single costume from start to finish. Something that doesn't require you to change between events. You can swim in the suit, jump on the bike and then run it.

However, in a race as long as this, I much prefer to get changed into the best gear for each event (which in Scotland, is a waterproof jacket) and, most importantly, change my socks so that I have fresh feet for the bike and run. It's amazing the difference a fresh paid of socks make. It's like getting pillows for your feet.

I put my tri-suit back and promise myself that I will wear it next time, even if it's just to catch the eyes of fellow triathletes.

SUNDAY 5 MAY 2024 (RUN)

A trail run in Arrochar and I'm running with another Celtman in training. Of course, of the six of us running, we're the two who end up lost. According to the t-shirt I was wearing, before I changed into my run gear: "Celtman XTRI: If you get lost, you are a moron."

I am a moron.

MONDAY 6 MAY 2024 (BIKE)

Today is a Bank Holiday so I start by getting up a 615 to get a few hours on the bike before everyone else is up and about and then, later, I get another long ride when I have the house to myself. Monday's are meant to be rest days. So are Bank Holidays. Not today.

TUESDAY 7 MAY 2024 (REST)

But today is a rest day. I needed it today after a busy weekend.

WEDNESDAY 8 MAY 2024 (REST)

Running Man Flu
Noun

An illness such as a cold that is incredibly serious, almost certainly life threatening, with just a touch of the sniffles, but the person who has it ignores it and runs anyway.

"Andrew has a touch of running man flu but he will be a complete hero and race on Sunday."

Last night I could feel a cold start, my nose fills up, my sinuses expand, and, just like the movie 'Grease, I can feel my temperature rising. Today, I'm working from home and I'm hoping for my cold to pass quickly so I can run the Loch Leven Half Marathon on Sunday.

THURSDAY – SATURDAY 9 - 11 MAY 2024 (REST)

Out of action for a few days as I chose the sensible option of dealing with my cold rather than trying to continue with my training. It's frustrating to have to stop for a few days when the race is next month but, in terms of timing, this was always going to be a tricky week as I had an event in Edinburgh on Friday night and a busy Saturday which meant I wouldn't have had much time to train anyway. So, instead, I worked out that I would make a brilliant junkie.

I was listening to an interview with the US comedian John Mulaney and, in it, he described how he would start the day with one pill, follow it up with another 45 minutes later and would then manage the ups and downs of his mood with a careful cocktail of drugs for the rest of the day. It sounded tiring until I realised it was exactly how I deal with a cold.

I start in the morning with two blasts of Sinex up each nostril so I can clear my nose and breathe clearly for a few hours. I take two aspirins, use Lemsip, have a Strepsil every hour and repeat that throughout the day until it gets to evening and I time all my pills, sweets, liquids and spray so that, at 11pm, I can finish the day with another Sinex to clear my nose to breathe in bed, and Night Nurse to knock myself out. If it's hard work being a junkie, then it's hard work managing a cold.

SUNDAY 12 – SATURDAY 18 MAY 2024 (BIKE, SWIM & RUN)

Very easy sessions to see off the cold. It can be frustrating in days like these to be running, riding or swimming far below what you think you should be doing. In particular, as May should be the hardest months and these days should be among the hardest days, I'm working easier than my initial days in January. But, to do more, would be too risk losing even more time. And it's better to be sensible and take it easy than to risk everything on trying to do more.

When I started running at university I would run on a treadmill for 20 – 30 minutes on a Monday, Wednesday and Friday. Over a year it became part of my weekly routine as I was studying for my final exams. Then, one day, my knee hurt.

"That's nothing," I thought. "A wee run will fix that!"

I'd pop up to the university gym and, after five minutes, the pain would start to fade, and, after 20 minutes, it would be gone.

"See," I thought, "it was just a wee niggle!"

And by the time I'd have my shower, my leg would fall off.

Not literally. I'd topple. But it might as well have as I couldn't use it for the rest of the day. It wouldn't bend. I couldn't put weight on it. I would hop from gym to library to home until...

I'd wake up in the morning, my knee would hurt and I'd think:

"Really, it's nothing, a wee run will fix this!"

And I was a cripple for a month until I realised that a 'wee run' will only fix this if your problem is an escaped lion and you need to get away fast. If your problem is a damaged ligament then don't run on it!

You need to follow the RIC (Rest, Ice and Compression) program not the RIC (Run, Ignore, Crawl To Bed) program.

Yet, 25 years later I've learnt nothing. Last year I pulled a muscle in my abdomen. Not sure how, think it was twisting to lift something while sitting in my chair at work, however, when I noticed it was sore, I thought immediately:

"It's nothing, a wee swim will fix this!"

And I went swimming. An exercise that requires you to continuously twist and turn.

Because there's nothing like putting out a fire like pouring more oil on it and shouting "Burn, baby, burn!"

It was stupid.

And, a couple of days later, I ended up in the minor injuries clinic complaining that I couldn't turn my body to the right or pick up any weight with my right hand.

Which was also stupid because, despite being a clinic for minor injuries, the doctor listened to my story and immediately said: "We don't do abdomens."

Which made me think: "What do you do? Left ankles only. Just the right elbow? How can you distinguish between different parts of the body? You're a doctor, your meant to do everything."

He sent me to my GP who's sole advice was "If it hurts when you twist to the right then don't twist to the right!"

Genius.

But she was right because she was just telling me what I already knew – if you're injured, then don't do twice as much as you did before in the hope that more means less. Rest. Ice. Compression. And don't go for a run. Or a swim. Or ride a bike.

SUNDAY 19 MAY 2024 (RUN + SWIM)

Up at 6am for an early start to complete a long bike ride. I'm standing in my cycle shorts, cycle top, in my cycle shoes and I've even sprayed myself with sun cream in case yesterday's good weather repeats. And it is then, and only then, do I realise that I don't have key for my shed and I cannot get my bike. D'oh!

I'd left my keys at work, and I had no way to open the shed without them. I had to change plans so stripped out of my gear and into a wetsuit instead, though not straight away, I still had to drive to a loch.

And, because I was missing a long run, I also decided to go for a run first. My day changed from a long ride to a run and then my first outdoor swim this year.

I'm never sure whether Celtman has a reputation for being cold because so many people don't swim outdoors in Scotland, and are used to 28 degrees of a swimming pool, or whether it has a reputation of being cold because it is cold. I view cold as being 12 degrees or lower. I'm okay with even going into the water to eight degrees. Below that, I then spend so little time in the water that it's not worth the time to drive to and from a loch. But 14 degrees, the average Celtman temperature, is okay. It will be cold, and, with an hour of swimming, I will feel it, but I'm not scared of it. It's just a normal temperature in Scotland.

Today was a chance to get used to the cold and that turned out to be a missed opportunity too as the temperature of the water was close to 20 degrees. Damn you, nice weather, why can't it always be cold and wet and miserable?

MONDAY 20 MAY 2024 (BIKE)

Another day of sunshine but I catch up with a longer ride by jumping on the indoor bike for a couple of hours. It gets harder and harder to complete the longer rides indoors. At least there's only a few more weeks to go before Celtman and I know feel back to 100%.

The problem with colds is that you're never quite sure when they are over. At least with an injury, it's obvious. I remember my first serious injury.

I knew it was bad when I started to cry. Not in a sad type way. More in a "AAAAAARRRRGGGGHHHH FLLLLIIIIIIPPPPPPPIINNNNGGGG NOOORRRAAA!" type way.

I was playing football and I knew as soon as I tried to tackle another player that they had a foot made of concrete and I had a foot made of napkins: strong enough to pick up pasta, not strong enough to build a house. There was only going to be one winner. I swung. He swung. He went right through me, and I fell. I didn't get up for three days.

When I hit the ground, I snapped a tendon in my ankle. I tried to stand, I tried to hobble. I even tried to carry on "It's alright, I'm okay!" I said (thinking I was a cyclist) but I quickly realised that you can't play fives while hopping on one foot.

Someone drove me home while the game continued but as I didn't have keys or my phone I was left standing outside my flat with no means to get in because I'd forgotten to bring my bag home with me. D'oh!

I then had to hop to my girlfriend (now wife) and hope that she was in.

I'm not sure what I looked like. Trainers, shorts, one legged and bawling but I do know that I saw no one on the way there. The same way that a charging lion doesn't tend to see anyone because all the antelopes run away when they hear it roar. Hop. AAAAAARRRGGH. Hop. AAAAARRGGH. Hop.

That night I tried to sleep but I couldn't even lay a blanket on my foot as the weight of even a silk sheet was like an elephant jumping on my foot.

"I think I need to go to the hospital," I said.

"You think," said the now Mrs CeltWife, looking very haggard after a night of failing to sleep because I kept screaming.

At the hospital a doctor confirmed I'd snapped an ankle.

"But I've got some good news," he said.

"Really?"

"Yes, you're in luck, we've just had an orthopaedic boot returned so you won't need crutches, instead you can wear a massive plastic welly with no toes that's impossible to keep your feet dry when it rains and it makes it look like you're doing a good impression of Robocop's leg"

(Not his exact words, but that's what he meant).

He then took out the boot.

"That looks like a moonboot," I said, trying to convince myself that it would be cool to be an astronaut and that my return to work would see me being asked:

"How did you get injured."

And I'd say: "Injured? Me? No, I'm off to the moon!"

But all the doctor said was: "A moonboot? Don't be daft. It's a surgical shoe."

Trust a doctor to ruin things by naming it correctly. Just like they spoil that innocent headache you've had for three weeks by calling it a brain tumour. The spoilsports.

That's why most athletes don't go to the doctor when they're injured. They'll only tell you that you're injured and that you must stop running. And no one wants to be told that. Instead, if you don't go to the doctor, you'll never be injured - unless someone snaps your ligament. Then definitely go and see a doctor.

TUESDAY 21 MAY 2024 (REST)

Travelling to Inverness and no opportunity to do anything today as I have a formal dinner tonight and I know I need to avoid having a pudding as I'm trying to be good and not eat any sweets in the run up to Celtman. However, cheese and biscuits can be a tricky choice too.

I once had Sunday lunch in Yorkshire: a warm inn on a dreich day as I tucked into a hot plate filled with slices of roast beef, vegetable and 'pudding' – the identifier Yorkshire being unnecessary in this plain-speaking Shire.

"Yorkshire puddin'? It's jus' puddin' round these parts! There ain' no other kind o'puddin'!"

And, for pudding itself (the sweet kind, not the suet kind, thus proving there is more than one type of pudding) I choose a selection of cheeses, because I was a triathlete and trying to be good.

"Do you have any biscuits to go with the cheese?" I ask, not unreasonably

"Of course," says the waiter, and then, unexpectedly, he pulls out a large flat drawer from a cabinet against the wall to my left, and places it with a flourish in the centre of the table; not batting an eyelid or pan lid at this impromptu act of dismantling dining room furniture.

"Enjoy", says the waiter, leaving the large drawer on the table; which I now see is filled with open packets of water biscuits, oatcakes and crumbly digestives.

How strange.

I can't help but wait until the waiter's back is turned before I peek into more drawers – just to check if they contain a similar surprise hoard of savoury snacks. I want to find a pork chop in a folio desk; a cabinet stuffed with nothing but carrots; or condiments in the cupboard, saucy and secret. But, sadly, they are empty.

I wonder if this is what Ann Summers means by 'edible drawers' but I don't want to go into one of her shops to find out.

But why are all the biscuits contained in this drawer? And why bring the drawer out and not just the biscuits?

Perhaps I was witnessing the act of a snack-aholic. Hiding biscuits away in unusual locations so that no one knows exactly how bad their snacking has become. A real crack(er) addict.

Or perhaps the drawer was just a marketing gimmick, a unique way of making you remember the meal long after the taste has long been forgotten.

Remember that restaurant in Yorkshire, you'll say.

What restaurant?

The one with a drawer filled full of biscuits.

Oh, that one. How delightful and quaint. A meal that was – *groan* – truly top drawer.

Anyways, I tell this story for one reason only – watch out for savoury snacks, even when you're trying to be good, always order a proper pudding.

WEDNESDAY 22 MAY – FRIDAY 24 MAY 2024 (WORK)

Work before work. Work during lunch. Work after tea. Repeat. Sometimes you must accept that life and work comes first because... well... Celtman doesn't pay my mortgage.

SATURDAY 25 MAY 2024 (BIKE)

Longest ride yet. Made even longer by watching a turgid Scottish Cup final between Celtic and Rangers. At halftime I bet £10 the game would end in a 0 – 0 draw and extra time would be required. After Adam Idah scored in the ninetieth minute for Celtic I was glad Celtic would win the cup and not sorry at all that I'd lost £10 as it also meant I wouldn't have to watch another 30 minutes.

During the ride, I checked out the route maps for each of the Celtman events. It always seems strange to check the route map for a swim. It's the sea, it's not like there is a route. You just need to know where to start and where to finish. But it was useful to see how the swim split into three sections. One kilometre to get to a corner of land where you can see the island in front of Sheildaig. Another kilometre to get to the island and then the rest to get around the north of the island and into Sheildaig itself. This final section was like the end of last's year Celtman solo swim route, so I know what to expect when I get there: jellyfish.

SUNDAY 26 MAY 2024 (SWIM)

In the office today. Our financial year is 31 May and there's a lot to do for it. I always knew this week and next would be hard, but I'm pleased to have at least got a longer ride in, even if I've not been able to fit in the runs during the week that I would have like to have done. I'd also skipped Thursday's swim, as I had to be in the office early. Today was a chance to catch up on the swimming.

MONDAY 27 MAY 2024 (RUN)

A longer run to catch up on running too. As I ran I thought about the Celtman run course and how I would feel after finishing the bike. I know that it always feels slower to start running, which is natural when you switch from 20mph on a bike to 7 mph on foot (at best, for both!). It doesn't just feel slower, it is slower.

I tried to run at a pace that felt comfortable and deliberately slower than I've run the last few weeks to try and get into the mindset of "I could be faster, but I'm not".

I don't know if this will help when it comes to Celtman, but it did lead to a very pleasant run as I ran into Pollok Park and had a nice sunny evening, the beauty of the park, and the sight of the Highland Cows in the middle of it with their new calves

TUESDAY 28 MAY 2024 (REST)

Another busy day at work so no chance to do anything. Instead, logistics. I've ordered more food for the race, this time a box of flapjacks I really like. For the race, I'm planning to have gels, flapjacks, jellys, energy drinks and a cheese sandwich.

Why a cheese sandwich? You can buy a synthetic gel that tastes like a banana. You can buy a bar made of nuts and grains that tastes like a chocolate cake. You can't buy a banana that tastes like a chocolate cake, but, with advances in sports nutrition, it won't be long before you can. However, it is pointless, because sports gel and bars are all about disguising what you're actually eating.

Who wants a gel that's a Bakewell tart or a bar that's pretending to be a strawberry cheesecake? Manufacturers should be honest and describe things accurately. I'd much rather choose between "Chalk", "Superglue" and "Smell Like Boak". At least then I'd know what I was buying.

That's why I loved the Rader Ride 2016, a bike race crossing Dumfries & Galloway and the Scottish Borders. Instead of the usual selection of gels and bars it had read food at its feed stations. It had everything: cheese rolls, ham rolls, cheese and ham rolls. You name it (as long it involved cheese and/or ham), it had it. It had also home baking with flapjacks and banana bread and great treat like Jaffa cakes and jellybeans. And, for those that wanted a banana that tasted like a banana it had a banana.

This buffet was my downfall.

At the end of the Radar Ride, you cycle a service road to a radar station above Wanlockhead. It's 2.5 miles of pure climbing culminating in a stunning view of Dumfries. But, at the bottom, they had a food stop – and I couldn't resist it. I just had to have another cheese roll. I stopped. Iain Celtbrother stopped. We shared a roll and then, with the road immediately ramping up, I was in the wrong gear. I had to push off a number of times to get enough speed to turn the wheel and change my gear but It was too late. Iain was already 100m up the road. He might as well have been at the top of the hill. I couldn't catch up.

But I'd had cheese, so I was happy. Because not only is cheese my favourite food it also helps reset your palette when you've had lots of gels. When I'm sick of sugar, when I can't face another slimy hit of synthetic Bakewell tart, a small bit of cheese make my stomach forget about everything it has and. A cheese sandwich is therefore a vital part of this long-distance athlete's food plan as it resets my tastebuds. And it's very, very tasty.

WEDNESDAY 29 MAY 2024 (BIKE)

At this point my easy rides match the hardest rides from the first few weeks of training. Looking in the mirror I can see a difference in how I look: thinner, brighter and more 'athletic', which is a polite way of saying gaunt.

I'm now ticking off sessions where I think "I won't be doing that again.". I can't imagine I'll ever spend several hours on an indoor bike again. This was a one off for Celtman, not a whole lifestyle changes where I swap my legs for a static bike. However as thoughts drift to what happens after Celtman, I keep forcing myself to stop thinking beyond it. I am training for Celtman. I want to complete Celtman. I'm not thinking of other races, events or event training after 16 June. Celtman is number one.

Except for work.

Which is why I'm up again at 630 to cycle indoors so I can get the session finished before I start work all day and all night, only finishing at 11pm.

THURSDAY 30 MAY 2024 (SWIM)

And up again at 5:50am. Even with a long day again ahead, I join my swim session.

"How long until Celtman?" I'm asked.

"Two weeks Saturday," I said.

"And how do you feel?"

"Better if we're only doing short and easy swimming today!"

FRIDAY 31 MAY 2024 (BIKE)

Finished work at 12:30am, woke up at 5:55 and back on the bike.

I always knew this week would be stressful as I've been working on projects that need to complete today and that it would be hard to fit training around work; but I hadn't expected to also be training for getting up early for Celtman too.

CHAPTER 10

CELTMAN SOLO POINT FIVE 2023

"It's not cheating if you change your shoes," he said.

I was at the final checkpoint of Celtman Solo Point Five, three miles from the finish, and a marshal was explaining that one of the fastest men stopped here and pulled a pair of trainers out of his rucksack.

Celtman Solo Point Five is a middle distance extreme triathlon with a sea swim in Sheildaig, a challenging 56 mile cycle around the peninsula (and up the Bealach na Ba) and a trail run along part of the Celtman run course and around Beinn Eighe.

The Marshall continued: "Even though he used 'cheat shoes', it wasn't really cheating. There's nothing in the rules against changing your shoes".

The Marshall went on to describe how one of the top competitors had worn trail shoes for the previous section of the race (an eight-mile track around the base of Beinn Eighe, before stopping at the checkpoint to change for the last three miles in:

"Cheat shoes." He said, "You know, just like Kipchoge's. The ones with springs for heels that make you run as fast as a cheetah."

"A cheetah?" I asked.

"No," he said, "a cheater, like Michael Johnson. Or that woman who took a taxi while running 100 miles. A cheater. Except there's nothing in the rules to say he couldn't change his shoes. So, you know, fair play to him."

I'm not planning to wear cheat shoes for Celtman like the Nike Vaporflys, with their special foam sole designed to give you added bounce, like running on a trampoline. But I am changing my shoes as today is New Shoe Day.

It's New Shoe Day because I always buy a new pair of trainers in the Spring sale – and always the latest sale model of the Asics GT 2000. Never buy the newest of the new trainers: save money and buy ones that are a year old. You'll still get the most up-to-date version, just 12 months later. How much can trainers change in a year anyway? Would spending extra money change the way I run? Or would it lead me into an arms race, or footrace, where only the best and newest technology will do? How long before I'm swapping shoes mid-race just to gain a small advantage?

"I asked him if it was worth it, changing his shoes. He said he would run at least five minutes faster in just a few miles," said the marshal.

And I thought: "Sign me up!". Well, at least for last year's model from the sale bin...

But not yet. This will be my final attempt at Celtman. And last year I entered Celtman Solo Point, also known as Baby Celtman, half the distance of the main race. During Baby Celtman, I met the marshal and listened to his trainer-swapping story. At this point, I was second-last, so even a five-minute advantage would have made no difference. I'd nearly broken my foot in training and was glad just to have made it to the start line – and even happier to have nearly made it to the end line without injuring myself again.

And, because I took part in the Celtman Solo Point Five, I qualified for a lottery to win a place in Celtman itself. 30 people are randomly selected, and I was one of those lucky/unlucky winners, even with a wooden spoon instead of fancy boots.

So, this year, instead of cheating, I have done the next best thing and trained instead. Who needs trampolines on your feet if you have rockets for legs? But's now May and in one month's time, on the start line, I might be looking for every advantage I can get. Today, however, I'll buy a new pair of trainers. I'm just sorry I can't also buy new knees in the sale.

Last though it wasn't knees I needed but a new foot. As I discussed last month, I managed to break it like Beckham and developed a metatarsal injury.

I was nervous about taking part. And the early start didn't help to calm my nerves.

Even though I was staying in Sheildaig, I was getting up at 3am. Baby Celtman is meant to be a triathlon. But, with a 3am start, as bags have to be dropped off with organisers by 4am, it should have an extra leg of "Getting Up In The Middle of Night" alongside the traditional swim, bike and run.

I say "getting up in the middle of the night" but as the race takes place two days after the shortest day of the year, it's likely to still be light at 3am. No wonder the organisers didn't include a head torch as mandatory kit for the run, it won't be needed, even at midnight.

As I said, the race has come after a spell of illness and injury including six weeks of not being able to do anything, so it was very much a case of turn up and see how far I could get round. It would be slow. There were cut offs to watch out for – but I needed to make sure I don't injure myself again.

The forecast was looking decent, with some rain forecast, and a tail wind for most of the bike course, which would be much appreciated by this injured competitor.

And I was nervous. I'm usually nervous before a race but these nerves were different. These were based on a lack of training rather than a fear of the unknown.
It's okay to be scared of the unknown. Who knows what might

be there? I've seen the Amazon Prime and Eddie Izzard film 'Get Duked', the Highlands are filled with rich lairds shooting tourists for fun .Who's to say the local lord wasn't going to pop out with his shotgun and shoot triathletes like grouse?!?

But to be scared due to lack of training is not okay because the fear is entirely self- inflicted. Like taking a shower in the laird's house without asking and then using all his best towels while singing "I'm the King of the Castle, you're the dirty rascal!" Of course he's going to react. Who wouldn't?!

But my lack of training wasn't entirely self-inflicted. I hurt my toe in Easter and couldn't run. I'd also picked up a chest infection which kept me out of action for another few weeks before hurting my chest and losing more time. In the run up, I'd lost more time than a careless Rolex salesman.

In the two weeks before the race, I'd finally had a run of days to train for the race and managed to run four times, cycle four times and swim twice. 10 training sessions. None longer than an hour. And I was then taking part in Celtman Solo Point Five, the 'Baby Celtman', a middle-distance triathlon based around the Applecross peninsula on the west coast of Scotland.

So, naturally, I was nervous until I had a simple thought. It went like this. "How will I do?" I said to myself. "Awful," I answered positively but realistically. "Oh, come on," I said, "it can't be that bad, at least you won't come last!" And with that thought I had a goal. I wouldn't come last. Second last maybe. But not last.

And how did I do? Well, let's just say if they had a gold, medal and silver for the last three places in the race then I just missed the loser's podium. (I was fourth last).

But let's start at the beginning...

Registration was open on Thursday PM and all-day Friday in a hall in Torridon. It was easy to find, and everyone was friendly and helpful. You need to bring certain mandatory run equipment (such as a waterproof jacket, hat, gloves, food, waters, first aid etc) and these are checked to make sure they are suitable for the race. Having run the route before as support last year I knew how horrific the weather could be for the run route. I'd brought two versions of everything. A run jacket for normal rain, the one I'd run around Glasgow wearing. And an industrial waterproof jacket for working on a trawler in a storm in a tidal wave. That way I could use either depending on the forecast. Luckily, while the forecast was for rain, it was to be mild rather than biblical.

The Celtman 'shop' was also open in the hall so you can buy your Celtman merchandise. I bought a t-shirt which had the slogan "If you get lost, you're a moron."

Little did I know how accurate this t-shirt would be...

The swim route started in Sheildaig and required us to swim round an island and back. Some warm weather over the last few weeks meant the sea swim was warm, with temperatures around 16 degrees. This also meant the water was suitable for jellyfish and there were plenty around the northern end of the island. I tried to swim further out to avoid them, which worked, but I couldn't avoid all of them and I just had to bat them away while swimming.

The swim start is early – 5am – and you need to drop off your run bag, set up your bike transition and collect your tracker before 4pm, though it looked like most people registered after this.

If you are driving, while there is plenty of car parking, it's at the other end of the village so you will need to park, walk to the transition and pick up points and factor in the time to then walk back to the swim start.

Again, everything is well organised, and it was always clear what you need to do and where you need to go. And what about the jellyfish, are they as bad as people say?

Celtman is famed for its jellyfish and many people are worried about swimming among them and getting stung. For most of the race I would have said "don't worry, they're annoying but you soon get used to them. They're only around for a few minutes of the race and most of the time the waters are clear and calm." And then, on the way back to shore, with around 200 metres to go, I was stung by one of the [expletive deleted]!

AAAAAAAaaaaaRRRRRRrrrrGGGGGGGGHHHHHhhhhhHhhH HHHH! Like getting a whip to the face from Indiana Jones.

The bloody [expletive deleted]!

And I could feel it for the rest of the face. A burning across my cheeks and mouth.
And while it wasn't painful, it was annoying, and I can't say I enjoyed it. So, if you don't fancy the idea of jellyfish then other races are available...

And did you come last? Not yet. I was happy with a steady swim around the island and a time of c45 minute. And, as usual, even though we weren't swimming together, I ended up climbing onto the shore just 10 seconds ahead of I was nervous Celtbrother. We must have been swimming the same speed all the way round.

A decent start but last place was still in my grasp as the next stage was going to be only the third time I've cycled outdoors in the last year. Would injuries, illness and a training program entirely based in Strava help me keep pace with the leaders? No chance.

The cycle route was 54 miles from Sheildaig, around the Applecross peninsula and back to Torridon. It involves more climbing than the full Celtman course and includes the famous Bealach na Beag mountain pass. The UK's highest road and one of the few roads in the UK with Alpine like switchbacks.

But it wasn't the climbing that I was worried about, it was the descent. I hate cycling down the Bealach to Applecross. A few years ago, a friend fell off the road and broke their shoulder, collarbone and wrist. Admittedly, they'd not checked their brakes before cycling but it has put me off cycling there ever since.

It was raining as we left Sheildaig for an eight mile stretch to the bottom of the Bealach. This was a good warm up to get blood pumping into the legs before the harder climbing begun.

I'd cycled it a few days earlier (one of my three outdoor cycles this year) and I knew what to expect. A steady climb and then an equally steady descent to the Bealach.

The rain stopped as the climbing begun and while clouds were down, and there was no view once we got to the two thirds point. The road is closed to traffic and it's good to just put your head down and grind your way up the road knowing there'll be no traffic coming in the opposite direction.

The first half of the climb is relatively easy, the second half ramps up. I was slow but steady all the way up and my hours on Strava had left some strength in my legs. Who says computer games are bad for you?

On the way down, I kept my brakes on for most of the descent and the squeals from my wheels sounded like someone had just jumped after seeing a mouse all the way down to Applecross.

The next section of the race, around the peninsula, has more climbing than the Bealach, but is spread out over more miles. I've cycled the route before so knew what to expect but if you've not done it then it can be tough to find you're going to climb more on what should be a flat section than you do on the climb. But that's the west coast of Scotland for you. There are no flat sections. Everything is Jack in the Box: up and down.

On this section, Iain Celtbrother punctured twice. He asked if I had a spare tube. I said he was a spare tube, he asked again and I said no, as I use a tubeless tyre, I didn't carry a tube. And, with that, his race was over, he had to call his wife to collect him so I thought like the concerned good brother that I am: "haha, well, after that, at least he'll be last!"

I was wrong. I finished the cycle without ever pushing myself too hard. As soon as I hit a hill I dropped to the lowest gear and worked my way slowly up it. I didn't see anyone until the last five miles. Between waiting for Iain and taking my time on the bike, the race was now taking place ahead of me.

At the run, I texted Iain Celtbrother to say he should pick up his kit and run with me. He could catch me at transition.

That's if I could find transition as I almost immediately got lost when leaving Torridon.

I don't know how I did it, but I was running along a road when everyone else was on a track. I saw a runner; he shouted I was running the wrong way and I climbed a bank of heather to join the track he was on only... I got lost again.

I came off the track at a point I thought it joined the road. It didn't. But I didn't know that as I climbed from the shore up through the forest at the side of Torridon and to the transition into the lower route around Beinn Eighe. Except I came to the transition after the exit to Beinn Eighe, which I knew couldn't be right. You had to go to transition and then go to the exit. You didn't go to the exit first.

Again, I was lost. The Marshalls helped by contacting the organisers who confirmed I should keep going. I wasn't the only one who'd taken a wrong turn.

Iain Celtbrother on the other hand had taken the right way and had caught up with me. We were able to leave transition together.

The lower-level route had a cut off time of eight and a half hours from staring the race. 1:30 pm after a 5am start. Our aim was to make the cut off. After that, there was no time limit to reach the end.

We ran most of the downhill stretches, some of the flats and walked the uphill. There was some rain but it was largely dry and conditions underfoot were okay. We saw a few other competitors the course ahead of us, and knew of one behind, who'd been at transition. What we didn't know was that these were the last competitors, we were competing for the wooden spoon. But first we had to make the cut off.

We thought the cut off was 10 miles into the race. This was a mistake. It was 12 miles. That meant we had to run all the way down the final descent to get in at 1:26pm. We thought we had more time as the distances were shorter, but we should have checked that more carefully before we started.

Having run the last part, we then walked into the finish, another three miles to Torridon. We could have run but as it was straight into a headwind and we wouldn't have run much faster than we were walking. Not even if I had changed in cheat shoes.

At the finish we finally broke into a run again and I finished ahead of Iain by a few seconds. I'd made it. I'd achieved my goal. I wasn't last. Iain was behind me, and even if he wasn't DNF'd for failing to finish the cycle leg, there was at least one other person behind him. Result.

Until we got the results and Iain was timed ahead of me! He was fifth last, I was fourth last. The b****ard.

However to make up for this. The next day I received an email congratulating me on winning a place in Celtman 2024…

CHAPTER 11

JUNE

SATURDAY 1 JUNE 2024 (REST)

Can you buy speed?

If your name's Jarvis Cocker and you sing that you're 'Sorted For E's and Whizz' then… yes…. yes, you can.

But, if your looking for speed and not a criminal conviction for class-A narcotics, speed can be bought legally. A race bike will be faster than a BMX. A pair of trainers will be faster than welly boots. Everything you wear or use can help you go faster.

Take bikes. Every bike is different. Even if you just look at race bikes you still get bikes which are better for climbing, better for sprinting, better for comfort or better for keeping your bum dry when it's wet. (I may have made that last category up, but, if it's not a thing then Specialised or Trek should make it happen. Who wants to go faster when it's raining? You just want a dry bum).

A TT bike on the other hand is the technical name for a smaller less comfy bike sold to big men on the basis they're sore back will make them think they're cycling harder but, and this this crucial bit, they also look cooler than a normal bike because you've got handlebars shaped like a unicorn.

Now some people might say that by sing a TT bike you're not actually faster, you're just merely buying speed by buying a different (faster and cooler looking) bike. But I like to think I get my speed the old fashioned way – no, not in a Lance Armstrong blood bag delivered by motorcycle courier – but through hard word, dedication, sheer grit and effective training.

Which is partly why I won't be riding a TT bike in Celtman. Instead, I'm going to use a race bike but with added TT bars. It won't be as fast as a TT bike but it also won't be as sore as a TT bike.

But more importantly I won't be exposed to the risk created by a typical Scottish summer day: strong gales.

I've ridden a TT bike in the wind and the wind would keep catching me and trying to push me over. Not only did it feel like have a parachute open behind me, my bike was a bucking bronco.

I don't want to spend 120 miles in saddle worrying about the weather, instead, I will use a rock solid bike and, when appropriate, some TT bars to give a little boost.

So, today, instead of training, I set up my bike so that I could use it tomorrow and see how it fits.

SUNDAY 2 JUNE 2024 (BIKE/SWIM)

Almost, was the answer. I need to angle the bars more upwards so I'm not twisting my hands down when holding on.

Good thing I'm checking this now and not at the last minute.

MONDAY 3 JUNE 2024 (RUN)

Kudos, according to the dictionary, is "praise and honour received for an achievement."

Kudos, according to Strava, is when you do anything. Walk to the shops. Take the dog out. Dip your toes on the beach. It doesn't matter what it was as long as you record it and add it to Strava. You'll then receive "Kudos" from your friends and followers when all they should be saying is "Why are you not doing any actual training?!??"

Maybe it's just me but even with normal day to day running or cycling, I don't want someone to give me 'Kudos'. I don't post any indoor bike sessions, unless I forget to make them private, for that reason. No one should get Kudos for sitting on a bike and watching YouTube videos. Kudos is for an achievement. It's not an achievement to watch Mr Beast.

Instead of Kudos, Strava needs new buttons to accurately record your reaction to someone else's post.

First, it needs a simple stick. Instead of giving Kudos to someone you see posting everyday, you should be able to click a 'Get Out Of Bed' button for someone you haven't seen post since last week. Imagining 20 people telling you to get a move on. That's motivation and far more likely to get you to do something than another Kudos.

Or, perhaps, if you have posted something, you need a 'Loser' button, to show you didn't think what they did was an achievement at all. A marathon? In lockdown? On your balcony? In the middle of a pandemic? Loser!

Or, even better, an 'I Did It Faster' button. Nothing inspires people more than competition. Of course, this button should be context specific. You couldn't tell your balcony marathon running mate that you did it faster last week because, unless you're a weird stalker, you weren't on his balcony for eight hours last week. At least, not running a marathon… This button would only appear if you are on a leaderboard with them and you genuinely went faster than them. If so, you can click the 'I Did It Faster' button. And then the 'Loser' button too to really rub it in.

Maybe, for a nicer approach, we could also have a commiseration button, just as Facebook has sad emojis. If you see a friend just miss out on a personal best or segment record then you can express sympathy.

Or you could also click the 'Loser' button. Your choice.

And that's it, that's what Strava is missing. It's missing a choice of reactions when you post an activity. It needs more than just Kudos and, if they did, if Strava were to add more button, I'd give them a big thumbs up.

Except today, as I forgot to charge my watch and had to work out my run afterwards by plotting the route on Google Maps and working out how far I'd gone. An important reminder though before Celtman: remember to charge everything electronic.

TUESDAY 4 JUNE 2024 (REST)

I feel I'm missing one long ride in training. I know why. I was ill for two weekends in May and I'd didn't get the rides I wanted then. My choice now is whether I should be catching up on that this week or whether I should be tapering. I keep changing my mind as to what to do. On one hand, it would give me a mental boost to complete the ride and to know that I did as much as I could before the race. On the other hand, would a long ride leave too much fatigue for next week? Would I be mentally ready but physically impaired?

I'm not sure of the answer yet.

WEDNESDAY 5 JUNE 2024 (RUN)

Checking the long-range forecast and it looks like it will be a typical Scottish summer day: some rain, some sun, and, thankfully, very little wind. Looking good, so far. I wanted to avoid strong winds so that the bike would not be a battle depending on which direction I was riding. I wanted to avoid a strong sun, as I'm Scottish and broil like bacon under a grill. And I wanted to avoid a downpour as I've already been through that when supporting Iain CeltBrother two years ago. So far it looks like the run should be dry and conditions will be better in the evening than in the morning. Overall though, it could have been a lot worse, and I'm happy with what it shows so far.

And in comparison, today was mild, then cold, then wet, then a deluge, then sunny. Good practice.

THURSDAY 6 JUNE 2024 (SWIM)

"Will this be your last swim before Celtman," asks the coach.

"I think so," I say, "unless you can bring some jellyfish to train with next week."

One of the other swimmers, a new guy, starts to tell me about swimming with jellyfish in Celtman Solo.

"Don't worry, they're just the moon jellyfish, they don't sting."

I don't tell him that I got stung by a jellyfish last year.

"Thanks," I say, "good to know!" But, from experiences, I'm assuming that they might and will plan accordingly. Which, now, is planning to brace myself for not using gloves. While Saturday's swim was easier, I think gloves and a watch cause to much pressure on my right forearm and wrist. I'll need to swim again with the gloves but without a watch to test this more.

When the session was over I swam another 600 metres to reach my longest pre-Celtman swim. While I've not swum as far as 3.4km, I've consistently swum further than in my previous long distance race preparation. To help with visualising the race, I was counting off landmarks as I swam. 900m before swimming towards the island. 1900 metres, I've reached the island and joined the course I swam last year for the Solo race. Once I've reached that I know the final stretch will be straightforward – except for the jellyfish. But they don't swim. Or so I've heard.

FRIDAY 7 JUNE 2024 (TAYLOR SWIFT)

Too excited to train. Taylor Swift at Murrayfield tonight and with a three and half hour concert ahead I don't need any more time on my feet. (But also shifting to only training two days and then resting to avoid fatigue).

Instead, I prepared an inventory of everything I'll need for Celtman:

SWIM	TRANSITION	BIKE	RUN- T1	RUN - T2
Hood	Towels	Bananas	Shorts	May (CM)
Goggles	Bike	Flapjacks	T-shirt	WP Jacket
Wetsuit	Helmet	Gels	Run bag	WP Trousers
Vest	Top	Cubes	Water bottles	2x base layer
Sandals	Waterproof jacket	Pretzels Coke	Gels	Whistle
Bus bag	Waterproof shorts		Flapjack	Headtorch (fully charged)
Water	Shorts		WP Jacket	Hat and gloves
Gloves	Socks		WP Shorts	Cheese rolls
Swim cap	Race belt		WP Hat	Hiking bag
Swim socks	Glasses		Ibuprofen	Water
Swim lube	Heat pads			Hiking sticks
Lens cleaner	Ibuprofen			First aid kit
Ibuprofen	Waterbottle			GPS (CM)
	Flapjack			Survival bag (CM)
	Four Gels			

	Pump			
	Saddlebag			
	Gilet (warm)			
	Waterproof gloves			
	Merino bike hat			

In previous years, I would have prepared this a few weeks ago but as I know I already have everything I need; I didn't need to prepare it earlier as I'm just creating a checklist to help pack. Not a checklist to help prepare.

Except, I did have to order one thing: hiking sticks. I know from supporting Iain CeltBrother that there is a steep climb from Transition T2A to get to the base of the trail around Beinn Eighe. While the hiking sticks won't help on the first half of the race, the ground is too muddy (if it rains) and the sticks will just get stuck in the ground and will only be useful if extended and used for pole vaulting, the second half is rockier, and sticks will help take some of the pressure from my legs.

And, even better, the second half is remote and it's unlikely I'll be seen. The first time I used walking sticks was on the Fife Coastal path. A largely rural path but with a couple of urban stretches that pass-through Kirkcaldy and Leven.

"Oi," shouted a man from a top floor window of his house, "are you going skiing?"

Ha. Ha. Eff off. We thought as we walked along the pavement in front of his house, our sticks click clacking on the pavement.

For Celtman, even if seen, we won't be mistaken for skiers, the worst that will happen is that we're mistaken for hikers, which, at that stage of the race, after the time cut off, I'll be quite happy to be mistaken for anyone moving.

SATURDAY 8 JUNE 2024 (BIKE)

Good practice for Celtman last night as 48 songs and three and half hours later (plus 30 minutes walking each way), I now know what it's like to be on my feet for the length of a marathon. Also, good practice for the cold as I started in a t-shirt, then added a second t-shirt, then a woolly winter jumper and then a closed puffer jacket. Not sure if Taylor Swift knew that Edinburgh in June can be as cold as Tennessee in Winter even when the sun is shining.

A longer bike ride this morning at an easy pace gave me a wee boost as I felt just as strong at the end as the start. So, Celtman only involves having to cycle sedately then I'm ready to smash the bike.

SUNDAY 9 JUNE 2024 (SWIM + RUN)

Another easy session, albeit a double one. I had a short swim and then ran four miles home. Again, both felt fine and if Celtman only involves a paddle and a gentle jog then I'm ready to smash the swim and run too.

Unfortunately, I undid all my good work by looking at the water temperature for next Saturday and getting the shock that it's looking to be a very cold June swim with some websites showing the current temperature as eight degrees Celsius.

To put that in context, eight, for me, is the point I quit open water swimming, it's not the point I jump in and start.

On the Celtman forum there's a post reminding everyone not to worry about the things they cannot control. And they're right, so I worry about the things I can control and one of those things is my wetsuit. I have a normal wetsuit. You can wear a thermal wetsuit. This is a wetsuit with an extra lining that keeps you warmer at lower temperatures. I've never felt the need to wear one as I've never needed to swim in condition where I couldn't control how long I would be in cold water. In a normal wetsuit, and wearing an extra vest, I know I can swim for 20 – 30 minutes. But Celtman will be at least 70 minutes, and, in the middle of the sea, there is no option of getting out and getting warm.

I spend a couple of hours reading reviews of thermal wetsuits. I keep changing my mind about buying one. The suits are expensive and I'm already paying a lot to race but, if it helps reduce the risk of hypothermia, then the cost would be worth it.

After a couple of hours of going back and forth, I make my choice. I buy a suit: a Zone 3 thermal wetsuit.

MONDAY (REST)

I start packing, using my inventory as a guide. Then add some more choices in just to be sure. I want to start packing now so that I can check what I have and what I might need from Iain CeltBrother. I don't have a first aid kit. Nor do I have a waterproof cap for the run. But I do have two wetsuits. Maybe I could wear both?

TUESDAY 10 JUNE 2024 (PANIC)

Do I buy a third wetsuit? Will it even arrive? Maybe I could get it sent to the hotel? But it's in Torridon and packages get delayed when you send them to the Highlands and, more so, when it's somewhere remote on the West Coast?

All these thoughts run through my head because when I tried on my new wetsuit, there was a small one-inch tear on the thigh.

I'm not sure if I caused it. I may have but I was trying really, hard not to do anything which would cause any damage. I was rolling the rubber, trying not to pinch or pull it and, still, there was a tear on the leg.

"I can't swim in this," I thought. The water will just seep in and negate any effect of wearing the thermal suit.

Instead, I wonder if I can return the suit, buy another on my credit card and have it here for Thursday before I leave. But, as this one arrived at 1700, I can't guarantee when it will arrive. It would almost definitely be too late for me as I leave in the morning, and too late for Iain CeltBrother as he leaves in the afternoon. That left the hotel. But that would be risky too as it may not even arrive on Thursday, or Friday.

Instead, I look at buying wetsuit glue but there's nothing on Amazon that will arrive tomorrow. The earliest anything will arrive, even with Prime, is Thursday. Then I remember that there is a wetsuit repair shop in Glasgow, Lomo, and I decide to take it there tomorrow.

WEDNESDAY 11 JUNE 2024 (Panic)

"Is that a wetsuit in your bag," she asks. Not a euphemism.

"Yes," I said.

"Sorry," she said, "our workshop is closed if you're looking for a repair."

So much for this idea. I buy some glue and need to DIY a fix. The first challenge is to read the instructions, which are printed very small in black on a yellow background on the tube of glue. I need to take a photo and then zoom into read them. While I wear glasses, and I know my eyesight has weakened, I didn't realise I needed a magnifying glass to read. Good thing there's no reading involved in Celtman.

The instructions are not very clear. Or at least not very intuitive. Use the glue on both sides of the tear. Wait eight minutes. Use it again. Wait for it to dry and then press the tear together. That doesn't make sense. You don't wait for concrete to dry before you pour it. You don't wait for mortar to set before laying a brick. Why do I need to wait for this glue to dry?

I try following the instructions and, later, when I try to stretch the rubber to see if the join holds, it does. But think how much stronger it would have been if I'd pressed it together when it was still wet.

However, I now have a thermal wetsuit and I also have some reassurance from the forecasts that the water temperature is currently 11 degrees in Torridon. A vast improvement on 8 degrees from Saturday.

The weather forecast is still for light winds and light rain showers so weather and water wise, the forecasts are looking decent.

THURSDAY 12 JUNE 2024 (TRAVEL)

Eat more and eat sensibly. The hunger has returned. My body demands food and I relax my 'diet' and eat a larger breakfast and include some more snacks during the day. I even have some chocolate again, which is good as Iain CeltBrother sends me a photo: "Tower of Snacks!" he writes.

And it is a tower of snacks. Plastic clear boxes filled with chocolate and sweets and gels and flapjacks and even Percy Pigs (I don't like Percy Pigs, but, after a few hours on the bike, I'll probably eat all of them).

How about a tower of drugs next, I ask/want.

Along with the boxes, Iain CeltBrother is doing a good job as supporter especially with an emergency bike repair needed today.

"You back tyre is flat," he phoned first thing.

"What do you mean? It was fine when I left it."

"All the glue is dried up and the tyre is coming away from the rim."

Which is the last thing I wanted to hear as we were packing to leave. I use tubeless tyres and the one worry I had about the bike was what would happen if I had a puncture. I can't change a tubeless tyre. If it punctures, it's game over. Back to the bike shop. But there was no time to take it in. I was leaving in an hour. Iain was leaving in two.

"What about another wheel? Can you swap in a wheel from your bike?" I ask.

"I can try but it may need a different gear as my set up is different."

I didn't even know this made a difference. I just assumed you could swap in any wheel.

"You can't," he explained, "the gears need to be the right size or the gears won't change."

Damn.

Then I remember I have a spare gear too.

"I'll bring a wheel too and the gear. You bring a wheel too and together we'll be able to sort it out."

Which was wishful thinking. When I checked for the gear I remember I would also need a special tool to take off the old one and replace it with the new one. I thought I had the tool but wasn't sure so I picked up everything I had that I thought was used to change it.

"I can't rely on this," I thought.

"Where are you staying tonight," I phoned Iain.

"Aviemore," he said.

"And when do you arrive?"

"4pm"

"Hold on, don't leave until I've called you back."

And I start googling and calling bike shops in Aviemore.

"Hello, I'm looking for a massive favour. I'm driving up the A9 today to take part in a race, Celtman, this weekend and I need help with a wheel. Would you be able to reset a tyre today if I brought it to your shop this afternoon?"

And the woman who answers resists the urge to call me a:

"Tube"

And says yes, bring it in and the workshop will sort it out today.

Iain texts at 6pm to share a photo of the restored tyre.

Now the only think I have to worry about is the front tyre. Maybe I should have asked them to do both, just in case.

And I should have asked about wetsuits…

FRIDAY 13 JUNE 2024 (SWIM)

It's cold, which is not a surprise. It's Celtman. The water is meant to be cold. But this is *cold* cold. The kind of cold that make you yelp when the water reaches your nether regions and gives you the singing voice of a Aled Jones and a flying snowman.

For this practice swim I've entered the water at Sheildaig pier, at the end of the village. A rocky slipway leads down into dark water. I've checked the temperature online and it predicts 11 degrees but as soon as I enter the water I think it's closer to 9 or 10. It has the feel of needles and the ability to slap you in the face and wake you up from even the deepest sleep.

I'm wearing my new wetsuit, which I notice has another small tear in it. All my panic for the last few days and there's still a tear in it. I know it's too late to do anything but it shows that I was right to just get some glue. Wetsuits will tear. This is a predictable as knowing open water swimming in Scotland will be cold.

But, to test the water, I start today without gloves or boots. I want to compare what it's like U2 style: with and without them.

And the answer is obvious as soon as I change. Wear the gloves, wear the boots. While it's not uncomfortable to go without, it's a lot warmer to use them. And with over an hour of swimming tomorrow I don't want to take the risk of starting without them, thinking it's okay, and then finding it harder and harder the longer I spend in the water.

I swim a few hundred metres, mind made up. I will use a thermal wetsuit, vest, balaclava, boots and gloves.

The rest of the day is spent at registration and then the briefing.

Registration opens at noon in the community hall in Torridon. We register early to try and manage to avoid any large queues. Before registering, the organisers carry out a thorough bag check to confirm that we have all the mandatory kit for both me and Iain as support runner.

We do. But only just. I checked the bag again this morning and spotted I'd misread the kit list. I thought we needed one compass between the two of us. Instead, both of us need to carry a compass.

I phoned Iain.

"Are you still in Aviemore?"

"Yes."

"Can you pick up a compass?"

The bike shop comes to our rescue again.

Registration is easier. I confirm my name, they confirm my number, we get stickers for the bike, bike helmet, supporter's car and transition bag, we get a pink supporter's t-shirt for Iain, worn to enter any transition area, and a sticker to confirm that Iain's vehicle is "Single support", which is not for Tinder, but gives access to a car park for the second half of the run course as support drivers who double up as support runners can park at transition.

The Celtman shop is also open. A series of wooden benches and trolleys covered in branded triathlon gear, t-shirts, towels, hats, caps and even a kilt.

In a couple of hours, the space is cleared after registration open, and it becomes a hall for the briefing. Attendance is compulsory and race number are checked to make sure you attend the right briefing. Numbers 1 – 125 at 3pm and 126 – 250 at 4pm.

The race briefing is the hardest part of Celtman. There are no seats in the hall, except for those brought in by athletes and their supporters, instead you either stand and lean against a wall or try and sit on the hardwood floor. Run. Bike. Swim. Sit. I would sooner do the first three than spend an hour on a wooden floor.

After 10 minutes, my bum is numb. After 20, my knees are complaining. After 50, I have lost all feeling in my lower body. If I wanted to do that, I would have stayed in the water.

The briefing is very useful and cover everything you need to know about each stage of the race, from where to go first thing in the morning, how to catch the bus, the routes for each part and any dangers to avoid.

I can't help comparing this briefing with the one I went to for Norseman.

For Norseman, the briefing started with Norwegian folk music. Then a film of the mystical nature of the race.

For Celtman, there was no music, only dick jokes.

Welcome to Scotland.

For a meal, we'd booked dinner at the hotel, and I had a burger. I don't know if it's the ideal meal before trying to get an early night's sleep but it sure was tasty.

After the meal, I switched on the Scotland game as they played Germany to open the European Championships. After 10 minutes and the first goal for Germany, Celtchild demanded the channel was changed to cartoons. I agreed and decided to go to bed. Luckily our room had black out curtains so as soon as I closed them it was midnight, even though it was 830.

I lay in bed, visualising the race in my head.

SATURDAY 15 JUNE 2024 (CELTMAN)

Alarm set for 245 am. Straight up, into the bathroom, where I'd laid out my wetsuit and the first task of the day required: lubing up.

A wetsuit is not the most comfortable or flexible clothing. Swimming for short periods of time is okay, but, for longer, I need to lube my neck and arms to stop friction burns. I don't want to be finishing the swim both cold from the sea and burning from my wetsuit rubbing my neck.

I also grab a quick bite to eat – a flapjack – and then meet Iain CeltBrother to drive to the start. We're only 10 minutes away, which is good, but when we get to Sheildaig there is a queue to park. The organisers do a great job of organising of directing traffic and directing cars into spaces so it's not too long before we're directed to a spot near Sheildaig pier.

"Do you have everything?" Iain asks as we walk to transition.

"Yes," I say.

But I don't. I don't have my swim cap. I need to run back to the car. D'oh.

It was damp when we got up but dry here in Sheildaig. The sun is starting to rise and the town is starting to show its colour. One of the cafes is open and there's a small queue outside: no athletes though, all supporters. No one wants a bacon butty before swimming two miles.

Transition is set up at the north end of Sheildaig. Racks placed in the middle of the street and access only for athletes and supporters with their pink t-shirts. I'm also wearing a big dry robe. And, like many people who wear them, I'm wearing it and I've not even been swimming. I guess it's okay though, I am about to swim.

We collect a GPS tracker and a 'dobber' from a small hall at the end of transition. Again, we queue, but only until we realise that the queue is for the toilet in the hall, not registration. Double d'oh.

The tracker, a small orange box, is left at transition. It will only be used for the bike and the run.

"It doesn't work in water," explained the organisers.

The tracker allows for people to track where we are on the online map. It would be good if it also had a button to add comments as otherwise supporters may get the wrong impression.

"Oh, he's going fast, he must be doing well"

But with a comment you can add: "The pain! The pain! The pain!"

The dobber is used to confirm when you enter and leave transitions. The organisers suggested having it around my wrist, but I change that to make it around my ankle. Later, one of the organisers says:

"I've never seen anyone use their ankle before."

I don't know why not. Having around my wrist is annoying when swimming as I like my wrist to be clear and it's annoying when running and cycle as the dobber wobbles. On my ankle, I don't feel it all.

The buses to the start line are above transition at the north entrance to Sheildaig. I say goodbye to Iain and find an empty seat. I think of sitting at the back like cool kids do, but, with a wetsuit on, there is no one cool on this bus. We all look like a rubber fetishists day trip to Margate.

"Where's the gimp?"

They're all on the bus.

A German man sits next to me. I know he was German because when he spoke, his accent was obvious.

"Congratulations," I said. Germany having whipped Scotland 5 – 1 last night in the Euros.

"Thanks," he said, "I wasn't sure whether to hide the fact I'm German today because of the result."

"Don't worry," I said, "we never expected to win."

The bus journey takes around 30 minutes to the start. It makes it feel like the start is miles away but the coastline bends back and forth more than a slinky so while it may be feel long, in terms of straight line distance, we've only travelled two miles.

At the briefing yesterday we were warned to watch our feet. The field is filled with sheep poo from the flock that we've shunted aside to make way for a flaming Celtman sigil, Highland drummers and 200 triathletes. I'm wearing my swim socks so don't care what I stand on, but, if you have bare feet, then probably best to bring some shoes or sandals with you.

You bring a bag to the start line, I brought a bottle of water, and there's a land rover to leave the bag so it can be brought back to the start for your supporter to collect.

I found a toilet. Well, I say a toilet, I copied the sheep had a wee in the field next to a tree before everyone was called over to the sigil for the lighting of the sigil and a photo of everyone standing in front of the flames. I could feel the heat from it but, with all my gear, I was starting to feel too warm. I hoped that I wouldn't feel the counter effect of that when going into the water: the water would feel even colder compared to how warm I felt now.

I didn't feel nervous. I was keen to get started. All I could think was to breathe deeply so as to adjust to any cold water shock.

We were called to the start and, as I walked to the shore, I met two other competitors from Glasgow Triathlon Club. One admitted that they hadn't brought their swim vest with them. I thought of offering mine because I was so warm, but I knew that would be a foolish move two minutes before diving into 10 degree water. Instead I said as we stepped into the water "It feels much warmer today," which it did. Unlike yesterday's swim, it didn't feel like I was slapped in the face as soon as I put my head below water.

The start of the race is on a rocky shower, so again, if you have boots, it's okay, but I imagine it would be uncomfortable to walk on with bare feet. The start is also filled with seaweed and kelp and you have to wade out 20 metres to clear the worst of it. Once clear, I was able to dunk my head to try and few short strokes to get used to the temperature.

I looked around to see how everyone was lining up. A short line was forming between two canoes. I waited for those who wanted to go to the front to swim past before joining the end of a line. I was quite happy to not be among the washing machine of the first swimmers and to hang back in cleaner water.

There was little time to think. From the shout to entering the water to getting to the 'start line' was around five minutes. I had no more settled than:

"Go!"

A shout. And we were off.

Head down. Right arm. Left arm. Breathe. Repeat.

The first part of the course is a swim from the shore to the left side of an island several hundred metres away. You then turned right and into deeper water to cross the sea to reach the left-hand side of Sheildaig island.

"For aiming," said the organisers, "aim for the white house on the shore that you can see just to the left of the island."

I stayed in that house last year. A fantastic location but with strange decoration. The living room had what can only be described as a 'shrine' to Spanish golfer Seve Ballesteros, who died over 10 years ago.

This was a rental. A home available week in, week out through the year. Why did it have a Seve shrine? Photos of the golfer and a frame that lit up to form one of the lamps in the living room. Who was hiring this house for its golf heritage? There's not even a course near here. Or anyone Spanish.

So, when we reached the island and started to turn, I couldn't help thinking of Seve as I spotted the house and started swimming back to Sheildaig.

Unfortunately, for most of my swim, I was getting a small amount of water into my left-hand goggle. Not enough to be annoying but just enough to make me close my eye as I swam. This meant, as I breathe to my left, every time I breathed and look out, I was looking with my right eye and couldn't get a good view of the land. I was swimming with an eyepatch.

I would stop occasionally to clear the water and to push the googles back onto my face. It never worked but it gave me a chance to look around and to take my bearings. Still facing Seve, still going in the right direction.

But to help ensure I was heading in the right direction; I would also try and find some feet to follow. Just like a bike, following someone has a slipstream effect, which makes swimming easier. And it has the benefit of not having to check direction, as long as you follow someone who knows where they are going.

To get the benefit of slipstreaming (slip-sea-ing in open water?), you have to swim quite close behind them. So close that if you time it wrong you tickle their toes with your hand. I would follow people for as long as I thought I was still in accidental touching territory and not seen as an underwater foot fetishist. Once slipstreaming turned into a kink, I tried to find another pair of feet to follow.

One of the challenges of swimming is that it's difficult to know how far you have swum and how long you've been swimming. I usually wear a watch when swimming but, in practice, I found wearing a watch and gloves placed more pressure on my wrist. When I had my practice swim yesterday I swum without the watch and it was a big improvement. Today, I'm also swimming without a watch which means that not only do I not know the time or distance, the swim also never happened. I can't record it, so I can't add it to Strava and if an athlete swims in the ocean without recording it on Strava, did it really happen?

(Yes, yes it did).

The Celtman swim is famous/infamous for jellyfish. Last year I was stung on the face but, this year, I only saw a handful of jellyfish as we crossed the deepest part of the loch. Thankfully there were none around the island and no need for Iain to get out the bottle of vinegar or, worse, his cock.

As I turned at the final island, and passed its westernmost point, I could see the end, the middle pier of Sheildaig. I could see swimmers stumbling out of the water, I could see the flames of the lit oil drums and I could hear the drums. I knew though from last year and from checking the distances again that while I could see the end, it is further than it looks to get there. The currant also become stronger and the water colder. There was a noticeable chill. Whether the cold and the current were in my head or real I don't know. I may just have been tiring. But it felt harder to swim forward and it felt colder in both my hands and body, which may me think the cold was real and not just cooling body temperature.

Towards the end, I kicked my feet and tried to get some life back into them. Remember how important it was to try and get the blood pumping again before trying to stand.

As I neared the shore, the drums became louder and the flashes of red and orange of the flames became more frequent. I wonder if this is what the devil thinks whenever he is summoned by a cult.

"Behold, hear the drum! Feel the flames!"

And then the devil pops out in a Zone 3 Thermal Wetsuit and says, "Thank God, my knackers haven't been stung by a jellyfish!"

A hand reaches out and pulls me up as I reach shore. There are volunteers at the edge who help me stand and I feel relief at finishing and happiness that I enjoyed rather than endured the swim.

Iain CeltBrother is here too, and he helps me along to transition. I pull off my goggles, balaclava and gloves as I walk. I don't feel cold and am grateful that I made the choice to wear everything. I'd much rather by bulky and warm than having to try and heat up.

"How was it," he asks.

"Swimming done!"

Transition

Iain has everything ready in transition. I use a towel DryRobe to strip and change and he passes gels and food for me to eat. The sun has started to peek out from behind clouds so it's a bright, warm-ish, and clam start to the day. There's no wind and, thankfully, no early morning midges. Around us, other athletes arrive and leave. Bikes are pushed along. Towels handed out. I don't see anyone shivering. Everything seems focused and orderly.

"What's the time?" I ask.

And am told 620. The swim was 1 hour and 15 minutes, which I'm happy about. I wanted to finish the swim and be leaving transition by 630 and it looks like I'll do that.

"Do you want the short shorts or the long shorts? Long top or short?"

"Everything," I say.

Although I don't feel cold, I'm wary of 'the drop'. This is when the warm blood in your body returns from your core and your core temperature drops. When you swim in cold water, your body protects itself by keeping your core warm. It reverses that when you start to heat up and you can feel your temperature drop.

I wear bib shorts with full tights, a base layer t-shirt, a lined long sleeve top, a Gillet and bike shoes with rubber waterproof boots. With temperatures predicted to be above 15 degrees even this early in the morning, I suspect this may be too much, but, just with the swim, I'd rather be too warm than too cold.

Iain has some milk, and I drink that instead of water. It's great to start the day with a different taste and it makes it feel more like I'm having breakfast than just eating for fuelling. It would almost be civilised, but no one eats breakfast wearing cleats.

I'm ready to go in 15 minutes and to start as planned at 630.

"Dobber?" I check with Iain.

"Yes, you are."

"GPS" I ask.

"In your pocket."

And I'm in ready to go. I put on my helmet, take the bike from the rack and walk to the end of transition and the line on the road that marks the point I can mount my bike.

"Ready," I say.

Mounting up. Getting set. Clicking feet into the pedals. And then –

- I wobble. I can't get my feet out. And I fall over to the left and bang my elbow and shoulder on the ground. The words of the organisers drift through my head:

"Only a moron doesn't start in the lowest gear."

There's a short steep road leading out of Sheildaig. The organisers had warned beforehand about making sure to start in an easy gear to get up the hill. I thought I had but, with this only being my second outdoor ride, this year, I'd got that completed wrong. My instincts kicked in and tried to change the gear only to hear the chain slip, my feet remained locked in the pedals and, before you can say "this is a terrible song by Pitbull", it was timber.

As I fell, I could only think about landing on my shoulder and not putting my hand out. I didn't want to break a wrist to start my bike leg. As I bounced on the ground, my water bottle bounced out and rolled away, but thankfully I didn't serious injure myself. Even was okay, except my dignity as just two seconds beforehand the presenter of BBC Scotland's Adventure Show had said "good luck, Andrew, you'll smash it!", proving that (a) he didn't know me, (b) he could read my name on my number bib; and (c) he was a nice man who just wanted to genuinely wish me well. At least he wasn't filming me leave, I thought.

"I got that on camera," said Iain.

Damn.

Bike to Kinlochewe

The first section of the bike race has a couple of undulating hills from Sheildaig to Torridon then a 10-mile stretch along the valley floor from Torridon to Kinlochewe. At this point there's plenty of cars trying to get past as supporters leave Sheildaig and try to get in front of their athletes. However, as a large stretch of the valley is single track it just creates a convoy of bikes and cars from Torridon onwards. The car cannot pass the bike and the bike cannot pass the cars. Everyone goes along at the near enough the same speed. It's only after we reach Kinlochewe that the road clears and normal riding started.

At this stage, with everyone bunched up, it was impossible to avoid mini pelotons forming. There wasn't enough space between cars and caravans to spread out. It felt like a fast start, but I tried to avoid looking at my computer as I didn't want to fall into the trap of checking my time or speed or distance constantly as, with many hours ahead, I knew the result would always be "not far enough, not fast enough, and nowhere near finishing".

The only thing I would do was glance my watch and check the time to see if I needed to ear. I wanted to eat something every 20 – 30 minutes. I had a feedbag on my top bar filled with gels, jellies and flapjacks. My plan was to keep it stocked up by replacing everything every time I saw Iain. I started eating with the flapjacks. Half a bar. Then a gel. Then back to the flapjack. Repeat for the rest of the day.

Kinlochewe to Gairloch

I met Iain just after Victoria Falls. Not the one in Africa. I wonder if Victoria even knew how many things were named after her and whether she ever said "wait a minute, we have one's the world's biggest waterfalls named after me, I don't need a stream in Scotland." I suspect the answer was never as today Victoria Falls is not just a waterfall in Africa. But with cultural awareness changing and bids to rename places with the original names, maybe one day Victoria Falls can revert to its original name of "That river with a bit of a drop", which sounds better in it's original Gaelic, where everything is named after what you can see. Big Hill? Ben (Mountain) More (Big). Say what you see geography.

At this point, I've been switching regularly between TT bars and normal riding. I was feeling good and with long straight roads with little elevation, it felt natural to make the most of the riding.

"Enjoy this," I would tell myself, "you'll never be here again on a bike!"

Which sounds fatalistic. Enjoy this and then you die. But I found it really useful to put the race into perspective. I had no intention of ever taking part in Celtman again. I know I won't be back here on a bike so I should feel lucky to be here today on a day when the sun was shining and there was not a breath of wind. Every green hill was like an emerald. Every blue loch shimmered. Everywhere I looked was a spectacular view. How could I not enjoy it?

Gairloch to Poolewe

I could be climbing for a start. The first quarter of the race is relatively flat. Gairloch, a small coastal town is the point that the route turns back inland and, to remind you that land exists, there is a large wall of it as you leave the town. A steep climb followed by some shorter climbs from here to Poolewe, a central town with a nice descent leading to an old Victorian bridge and a nice flat section beside Loch Ewe.

By this point I was looking for Iain again as I realised two things: first, my feedbag was too loose and swung left and right on my top bar. I constantly had to nudge it back to the centre with my knee. And, second, I'd lost my bike computer. Or, more accurately, I'd lost Iain's bike computer. It must have come off my frame at some point the previous five miles but I'd not noticed when it happened. I switch my watch's tracking on and started recording from here. I was annoyed to have lost the computer but as I was avoiding looking at it anyway, it made no real difference to my race.

"As long as I don't lose anything else," I though, remember the man who rode past about an hour ago and who then showered me in plastic fragments as parts of his bike exploded. I couldn't work out what had broken, and either could he. He was still able to ride, but there was a shower of small plastic fragments thrown up in the air and no idea as to why it happened.

"I don't need my computer," I thought.

Poolewe to Gruinard Bay

"But I do need my water bottle!"

It disappeared somewhere close to the bay. Just like my computer I don't know when it vanished. Maybe a phantom was taking it. A phantom who was now equipped to take on a long-distance triathlon. Casper the Friendly Triathlete.

While the bike route is spectacular most of the way round, this stretch is 90s boy band: another level.

The road curves back to the coast and hugs the spectacular west coast with crofts, machair, forests, hills, heather and beaches spread out before me. It also features the steepest descent of the day as a mile long descent from the viewpoint overlooking Gruinard Bay takes you back inland after teasing you with the finest views the NC500 can offer.

Luckily, I met Iain just after Poolewe and he had a spare water bottle. As I put in my holder I realised the crash had caused more damage than just to my dignity. The holder was cracked and barely held the bottle securely. It rattled as I rode. I'll need to keep an eye on it, I thought. Which I did, so I was able to see it shake itself loose and bounce down the road as I finished the descent from the bay. I stopped and turned round to pick it up. And promised to keep an even closer eye on it as the last thing I wanted to happen was to race the second half without any water.

Gruinard Bay to Corrieshalloch

In my mind, this was going to be the hardest section. It features two long climbs, one through trees and another across the moor before reaching Corrieshalloch Gorge, a narrow cleft in the landscape with a proper waterfall (Victoria, I'm looking at you).

By this point, mid-morning to lunchtime, I decided to swap to a short-sleeved t-shirt. It was getting warmer, the wind couldn't blow out a candle, and the sky was getting clearer.

I alternated resting on the tt bars with cycling normally. If flat or downhill I would use the bars. If uphill, I would cycle with my handlebars. The only downside of being on my TT bars was that I couldn't see the long views over the moorland to the south. Everything was tarmac.

The first climb was around three miles, and I just ground it out. With trees surrounding the road, it was hot and more suffocating. I stopped once with Iain to drink and told myself "get through this one and there'll just be one more climb to go. Then it's either flat or downhill to the end."

At the top of the climb, the road opens to the moor and there's a few long gradual descents to rest legs and get breath back. It was fast going, and I tried to enjoy it while knowing another climb was coming.

Until it didn't. I looked up. I was at the viewpoint for the gorge. Iain was parked and took a quick detour to see the view to the north, the gorge opening and leading into Loch Broom and to Ullapool. Mountains turning to moorland turning to croft land turning to shore and sea. Grey, brown, green and blue. All of Scotland rolled out before me.

I could see a car pass along a road on the hill across from me.

"Is that not the A835?" I asked Iain.

"Yes."

"What happened to the second climb?"

"What second climb? It's flat or downhill from the top of the forest."

I'd misremember the route. I was sure there was a second climb from the moor to the gorge but I was wrong. I was here. 45 miles to the finish. The climbing behind me and now a fantastic 20-mile stretch along the A835 to Garve.

Corrieshalloch to Garve

This is the section I've dreamt about. This is a road from home to the mainland. Every summer until I was 18 years old, we would get the boat from Stornoway and holiday for two weeks in Aberfeldy. This is the only road between Ullapool and Inverness so this meant that this road was the first time each year I would be on the mainland and free from the Isle of Lewis. Travelling south always felt like a release. So, when I thought about Celtman, I always thought of this road and the section beside Loch Glascarnoch, in particular. The loch ends is a reservoir and ends with a dam at its southmost point. The dam, to me, was immense. To me, it could have been the Hoover dam as it seemed to stretch across the loch and held back the Highlands. To cycle along it was to ride not just for Celtman but through childhood memories and the possibilities that escape felt like to a boy born on an island and always 11 months away from the bright lights of the mainland.

This section was easy and fast and apart from arriving at the dam and finding Iain completely unprepared with his back turned, staring out at the loch, it went smoothly and to plan. While there are a few cars on the road, it only appears busy compared to the quiet roads around the coast. Most cars are supporters passing. Currently, a few hours before the ferry traffic starts, there's not too many cars on the road.

Instead, head down. On the TT bars. Downhill to Garve and remembering the past.

Garve to Achnasheen

A right turn across traffic but there's plenty of time to prepare and plenty of space to see what's coming.

There's a quick climb and then a long straight line to Achnasheen. By this point, my legs were heavier, and I wasn't looking forward to another 20 miles. However, to help split it up, when driving along on Thursday, I'd marked points of the road in my head as target. Head to the loch. Pass the homes to the right. Into Achnasheen. Past the next loch. Descend to Kinlochewe.

I checked the miles on a road sign. 16 miles to Achnasheen.

"Excellent, only four mile to Kinlochewe once I get there – and they're all downhill."

About 10 miles in, I stopped for a final 'binge' from Iain's boot.

"I've got you a present," he said, "chips and cheese!"

And he held out a plastic carton with a fork stuck out of it. Inside was glorious chips and cheese.

"Better than an energy gel!"

The cheese was perfect. After 7 hours of eating energy gels and flapjacks, it helps reset my taste buds to eat something salty and savoury. I only had a few bits, not wanting to test my stomach too much, but it was just enough to give a great to the finish... except...

Bang! There goes my water bottle. Bang! There goes the car wheel over it. And, after I turn round and pick it up, I lift it up and all the water leaks from the cracked top.

"Oh well, at least it last 115 miles!" I thought.

Except it hadn't as, when I get to Achnasheen, a road sign says it's another 10 miles to Kinlochewe. I'd managed to get my route wrong again. And this time I've added back the five miles I saved on the moor.

Head down. Legs tired as they're now being asked to do more than they expected, and I start the last 10 miles to Kinlochewe.

For the first time, the wind has also picked up. It's not strong but I can feel a headwind so that when I reach the summit above Kinlochewe and start to descend the valley, I can feel it push me back and I must cycle more than expected.

The view around me is fantastic. A week of rain sees the valley sides glowing green and brown with heather and ferns. The road stetches two miles before me and Loch Maree glistens in the distance.

"Nearly there," I think.

Kinlochewe
And a change to the transition. It's no longer in Kinlochewe but a few hundred metres past it.

Iain greets me at transition.

"How was it?"

"One done," I said.

Then remember. Oh, I've also been swimming today. After

nearly eight hours on the bike, it may as well have happened on another day.

"Two done!"

Transition 2A

And after eight hours on the bike. Thank you. A portaloo!

The transition is beside the car park, which makes it easier for supporters as previous year had seen the two separated and supporters having to push the bikes along roads to get back to their cars.

There were a handful of people in transition, and it was still dry and clear but with weather reports of some rain I also grabbed my waterproof jacket along with my running vest. I also used waterproof trail shoes after people had reported earlier in the week that the first section was quite boggy.

Iain offered to run the first section back to Kinlochewe, which was good as...

Kinlochewe to Transition 2B

The change from cycling to running is always tricky. You change from cycling at 15 mph or faster and then must adjust to running at a marathon pace of 6 mph (or slower).

My legs also felt heavy as we left transition so it was good to have Iain run alongside as it forced me to run more than I would have if I'd been on my own.

The first section is along the Beinn Eighe trail. Largely flat with a good trail route to follow. The route circle round and then through Kinlochewe before joining up with another path leaving Kinlochewe to the west.

I say path. It was only a path to the extent that others had followed it. It was no more a path than Victoria Falls was a waterfall. It was mud. Just mud.

Iain stopped at this point so didn't see the worst parts of the path but for the for the next 5 km I tried to move as fast as I could, but it was only just faster than walking pace. Every step was an attempt to find solid ground, or at least ground that didn't swallow my foot.

To make it worse, it started to rain heavily, and I was glad that I brought my waterproof jacket. I raised my hood and kept squelching forward.

I knew I had over three hours to make the cut off at T2A for the low level route so time was not important. But I tried to go as fast as I could in this first section. I knew I had plenty of food at T2A and was walking the low level route so could use the last of my energy to get through this section as quickly as I could. I ran bits, power walked others and passed a few people trudging through the mud ahead of me.

After 5 kms, the path cleared and moved to a wide fire trail leading to a very steep climb. At the top, the rain finally stopped, and I was able to run down the hill and to the first support of the day. A table with some very wet biscuits and a couple of large drums of water.

"How far to the finish?" I asked.

"About 10 kms," they said.

Which was longer than I thought but no more than a hour and half away even at my slowest speed.

I continued to alternate running and walking (with the walking taking longer and longer each time) and enjoyed running along a loch and through a glen as I made my way back to the main road between Kinlochewe and Torridon.

At the road, after about 5kms it started raining again. A deluge of raindrops bounding off the road.

I kept my head down and just thought how, in another couple of miles I would be finished this section and able to dry myself off and change into fresh clothes.

"How far to the finish," I asked a man walking towards me.

He looked at me like I was daft. "It's there," he said, "pointing 100 metres ahead".

I must have misheard the distance before. I was expecting another couple of miles but to see the finish ahead was a relief, and, even better, looking down the road to Torridon, I could also see the skies were clearing and it would soon be dry.

"I'm there," I thought.

Transition T2B

"But where are you?!?" I asked.

I arrived at Transition T2B, a small car park at the base of Beinn Eighe, and Iain was nowhere to be seen. There was a small canopy set up to provide some shelter for checking bags and, hurrah, another portaloo, but beyond a few supporters and athletes bustling around and getting ready to leave, there was no sign of Iain.

"Where are you?" I phoned.

"I'll be there in a minute."

Five minutes later I can see my car on the road and Iain getting out. Has there been an accident? Has something happened to his car and he's had to be picked up by my wife?

"No, I went back to the hotel because I thought I had time to empty the car. I then thought there was no point driving back, if I could get a lift instead. As we could then avoid having to come back later to pick it up. But you were too fast!"

I didn't feel like it. It was around 2 hours 20 minutes from T2A to T2B. Originally, I'd hoped for around two hours but that was before I knew about the mud and before I saw how tricky the first half could actually be. In the end, I was happy with my time, and, having changed clothes into hiking gear, I was dry, I was well fed, and I was ready to finish the race.

"Did anyone leave their light?"

D'oh. That was me.

At T2B the organisers will check your bag to make sure you have all the mandatory kit. I had to take everything out, show it to the volunteer and they then confirmed I could carry on. Unfortunately, I'd not picked up my head torch when I repacked. Not that I was thinking I would need it but, knowing how bad it was last time with Iain, I knew how important it was to be prepared for the worst conditions.

T2B to finish

Ready to go. There is a short walk along the road to get to the start of the low level path. Then a steepish climb on a well worn rocky trail for a couple of miles to get to the valley that runs around the base of Beinn Eighe.

The organisers say not to confuse the low level route with an easy route. It's not easy. And they're right. In the rain, it's a technical and slippy route. Even in the dry, it has plenty of climbing and is a challenging route with a couple of river crossings and some short sharp climbs even on the level floor of the valley.

At the start of the first climb, I take out walking poles. While allowed, there is a unwritten rule to try and avoid using them.

"Remember to put them away if you're seen by the photographer," they joked at the briefing. But, at this stage, I knew the poles would help take some pressure off my legs and would make the last stretch easier. I had no second thoughts about using them.

My second boost was the one thing I'd been looking forward to all day. My one request for Iain was to have a cheese roll at the base of Beinn Eighe. And, when he picked up the chips and cheese, he also picked up my roll. That meant that when we came to the first rise, and looked back down the hill towards T2A, a few hundred metres below. I sat down and had a picnic. An XTri picnic. An Xpicnic? And it was fantastic. Finally, some proper food, eaten at the base of a mountain, with the sun breaking through the evening clouds. I could not have asked for a better meal.

From there, as the sun started to lower, the views along the valley were clear and bright and lifted my spirits as I contemplated the last few hours ahead. I had no doubt that I would complete Celtman. It was just a case of one foot in front of the other until it was done.

In the opposite direction, we could see runners and supporters coming towards us. These were the athletes who had made it onto the high-level route over Beinn Eighe.

"Congratulations! Well done!" We said as they passed, standing aside so as not to block the paths.

I wouldn't know what to do if I had to take part in the high route. Racing on a dangerous summit has no appeal to me. I was happy to be on the low route, but I admired all those who had made it to the high route.

We carried on, enjoying the hike and making no attempt to run. After an hour, we were passed by another athlete from the Glasgow Triathlon Club. She's been an hour behind me on the bike and was no overtaking us on the run. She didn't look like she'd been out for five minutes, never mind 15 miles across the mountains, or 120 miles around the NC500.

"I bet you've not had a cheese and ham roll," I said.

After crossing a small wooden bridge, the low-level route starts to descend toward the coast. First through a forest, then past a steep gorge, then into Torridon Estate to walk about the coast road toward Torridon. I thought there would be more midges at this point but thankfully apart from a few small spots, they were largely absent.

It was around 8pm when we could see Torridon and could see another couple of miles of walking to finish. The sky was starting to turn yellow and pink and it was a cracking night.

"I don't think I could have asked for better weather," I said to Iain.

"You could have had a hell of lot worse," he said, clearly remembering his own race. At this point, we'd been soaked to the skin even with strong waterproofs.

"Though maybe should have worn some suncream,"

"Eff off," said Iain.

As we neared Torridon we could see the athletes of the high course run as they approached the finish line with a final loop around the Torridon shore.

"Do you think we'll be confused for the high-level route?" I asked.

"What do you think?" said Iain, indicating our hiking clothes.

"Probably not."

As we walked through Torridon, the homes on our left, the sea on our right. I started to dismantle my walking sticks.

"What about now?" I asked.

As a high-level runner with oak thick thighs ran passed us.

"Still no." He said.

"But I should run to the finish too." I said.

And, with the finish line in sight, an inflatable blue arch with "Celtman!" across the top, I started to run the last 25 metres.

20 metres.

10 metres.

5 metres.

And...

"Thank you!" I say to the volunteer who offers me a Celtman beer.

"Thank you," I say to the volunteer who takes my dobber and GPS.

And

"Thank you," I say to Iain.

Post race

The hall is packed. It's warm and a queue for food stretches along three walls. But I'm finished. I'm happy. I just want to eat, get home and sleep.

Last time we were here the hall was nearly empty and the food was terrible. I suspect, due to the terrible conditions, no one stayed as they wanted to get home to get dry. But this time the spaghetti and meatballs are delicious and there's a great atmosphere as athletes and supporters linger.

"I'll call Mrs Celtwife to pick us up," I said as we finished eating.

"I'll be there in two minutes," She said, so we left the hall and started walking towards the hotel, thinking we'd be picked up any minutes.

10 minutes later we were almost at the next village when she

pulled up.

"I thought you'd be two minutes," I said.

"I through you'd enjoy the walk," she said.

And she was right. I did. The walk. The run. The bike. The swim. I loved every minute of it.

SUNDAY 16 JUNE 2024 (FATHER'S DAY)

I'm wide awake at 5am. No sleepy minutes as I open my eyes. I'm instantly awake as fast as a light switch. Not that it's light. We have the black out curtains, so I have no idea of the time, and, as I have no clock near me, I have to get up to find my phone and check the time. 5am. 24 hours later and my body is still saying "you need to race!". But my body is an optimist. My legs are stiff and sore and weak. I wobble a bit as I try to get up as muscles try and switch on but find the tank is empty.

I try and go back to bed but I'm up again before 7am having failed to sleep. Instead, I want food and, spotting a Tunnocks tea cake, I start the day with chocolate, and it tastes fantastic.

Today is Father's Day and Celtchild has a present for me a Peppa Pig book called "Daddy Pig's Big Fun Run", which would be a great name for a race. Never mind Celtman Extreme Triathlon, what about Celtman Big Fun Swim/Bike/Run?

Today is the t-shirt presentation, photo and ceilidh. However, as we're heading back to Glasgow, it's a very quick trip to the Torridon Hall to pick up my t-shirt and then back to the hotel to pack and leave. The organisers have breakfast for everyone with the smell of bacon rolls filling the hall. I can see a lot of people wearing warm puffer jackets and move carefully and slowly. We look like we're walking on the moon.

I don't feel any sense of achievement or pride when I pick up the t-shirt, I'm too busy thinking about getting back down the road. I don't even put the t-shirt on until I get home, six hours later. I'm proud of what I've done but, in the end, I didn't need to connect that to a t-shirt or a ceremony, nor do I need to be in a photo with everyone else. Perhaps if I had more time, I would have stuck around but, for me, I wanted to be home.

The drive home was slow, and we stopped in Aviemore for lunch. I wore my bright blue Celtman cap.

"You're not wearing that, are you?" Asked Mrs Celtwife.

"Yes," I said, "I'm entitled to wear it now! I am a Celtman!"

"No," she said. "you are a twat."

"But a twat that has completed Celtman!"

We then walked along the main street in Aviemore, turned a corner and almost walked into another man wearing the Celtman cap and his wife. I thought "he's a cool dude" and we both gave each other nods of recognition as we passed. Game meeting game.

"He had your cap," said Mrs Celtwife.

"Cool dude," I said.

"But you should have seen his wife's face. She was so embarrassed."

"Did it look like yours?"

"No, mine has more disdain!"

MONDAY 17 JUNE 2024 (REST)

The washing machine. Washing the wetsuit. Back to the washing machine. Another load. It's a good thing I've taken the day off as I need it to complete all the washing required to deal with everything from the weekend. Swim, bike, run, rinse, wash, repeat.

I could have washed my clothes faster but I only saw this tip later after I went to the sauna for an hour. There was only one other man there and there's a room in sauna which has heat vents on the floor.

"That's strange," I thought, "it looks like someone has placed a folder cloth over the vent."

I looked closed. He had a pair of swim trunks open over the vent and was drying them using the hot air from the vent.

"I think I'll go home," I thought.

TUESDAY 18 JUNE 2024 (ATTEMPTED BIKE)

A short 45-minute ride which, ouch, only, ouch, confirmed that while the mind was willing to try and get moving again the body still had so many chafes around my thighs that I might as well have ridden a razor blade. Ouch.

WEDNESDAY 19 JUNE 2024 (ATTEMPTED RUN)

I had 10 minutes to get from Queen Street train station to Central Station. I'll jog over to make sure I get my train, I thought. Something I've done many times before.

One step, two step. No. Not going to happen.

THURSDAY 20 JUNE 2024

If you complete Celtman then you are eligible for points which help with entering other extreme triathlon events. Celtman is part of a series of races under the XTri banner. If you pay a small annual membership then, for every event you complete, you are awarded points which can be used to bypass ballots in other races. I checked my points today and I now have enough points to enter any race without having to enter a ballot, including their flagship event, Norseman. A race in Norway that starts with a leap from a ferry into a fjord and finishes on a summit of a 4000m plus mountain.

Today, I struggled to walk up the two flights of stairs to my office.

ANDREW TODD

FRIDAY 21 JUNE 2024 (REST)

James Bond stands triumphant. Blofeld is dead. The nuclear missile launch has been averted and the world is safe once more. Bond is bloodied, bruised and mildly blootered after too many shaken and not stirred martinis. But he doesn't feel it – at least not until the next day…

When he goes to Tesco and buys some milk because the milk in the fridge went off while he was trotting around the globe; when he pops into the dry cleaners to remove the lipstick from his dinner jacket after a night with Blofeld's beautiful assistant; when he slumps in front of Homes for the Hammer and thinks "you'd think I'd have got more than one day off before I have to go back to work and sit at my desk and catch up with all the emails I haven't answered – I don't want to go to work tomorrow!!!".

Of course, he could skip work. But just because you're a commander of the British Navy and an MI6 agent with a licence to kill doesn't mean you can take your own holidays when the rest of the department has already booked it because it's schools week. You try not turning up for work. You won't be handed a Walter PPK again, you'll be handed a P45.

I love thinking about the day after. What happens next for the heroes and villains we read and watch? Did Robocop rescue a kitten from a tree the day after he brought down Omnicorp? Did Hannibal Lecter have a chicken pot noodle because he'd ran out of livers and a nice chianti? What does Darth Vadar do on his day off? Does he, like Boris Johnson, paint buses using cardboard boxes?!? What happens the day after?

No one ever talks about the day after because nothing happens the day after. The adrenalin is gone. The action is over. It's all admin, resting, cleaning up and blocking the number of the beautiful assistant from your phone as you don't want to accidently answer it after she betrayed you and tried to kill you with a booby trapped piranha tank.

It's no different from triathletes. Think about the day after a race. What happens then? You might have to travel, spending hours in a car with stiff legs and a sore back. You have to empty bags and wash race gear and wetsuits. You might check times and photos and update social media with all the ones where you have your stomach stuck in because tri-suits are not at all flattering...

Then the day after that, you think. What do I do now? You can't save the world every day, just as you can't race every day (unless you're the Iron Cowboy).

And without the adrenalin of a race, and without the goal of an event to train for, it's easy to fall into a slump. Why run, if you're not training? Why go out on the bike if not as preparation? Without a goal it becomes harder justify your actions. Swim in the morning and then run home from work? That was normal, one month ago. Now, what the blooming Nora were you thinking? Two showers in one day? How did you find the time!?!?!?

So, those first days and weeks after a race are a critical time. It's easy to forget training. (And, possibly smart to do so as you can't keep going at same rate after a race without risking injury). It's easy to eat cake. (It's always easy to eat cake!). But it's also easy to try and recreate the race high. It's why organisers know the best time to sell next year's race is the day after this year's race to the people who've just woken up with a feeling of invincibility like they've just saved the world.

Sometimes I think James Bond must be an Ironman triathlete as only a triathlete with the Ironman bug, would think "hey, I've saved the world and almost killed myself, but you know what would be great – doing it all over again and again and again!"

I'm sure the next James Bond film will feature him killing twice the number of henchman, bedding four times the number of women, while saying he really, really doesn't need a wetsuit because swimming to the underground lair in 10 degrees of water wouldn't be extreme enough if he didn't do it in skins.

After Celtman, I knew I would feel these thoughts. The need to chase the next adventure. That I'd want to look at the next race and the next hit and not just enjoy the feeling of completing Celtman itself. So, I made a promise to myself. I wouldn't enter or commit myself to anything serious for at least two months after finishing. Only then would I think about whether I would want to train for a long distance event again.

So, amateur athletes of the world, remember this – even James Bond can't save the world every day.

But at the end of every Bond film is the same message: "James Bond will return"....

OCTOBER 2024

I enter Norseman.

NOVEMBER 2024

I don't get into Norseman.

Phew!

Printed in Great Britain
by Amazon